Praise for
Happiness According to Jesus

"If you are looking for a positive message in this downbeat world then reading what Bobby Schuller has to say is just what you are looking for. He makes following Jesus a joyful journey."

> – Tony Campolo, PhD,
> Eastern University

"Common happiness slips through the fingers of our lives. The happiness Jesus offers, however, calls us, wakes us, heals us, recreates us, motivates us and directs us for lives of love and justice. This is the happiness of life we find in Christ and it cannot slip away. Bobby Schuller wants to make sure we hold this greatest of all gifts when Jesus Christ holds us."

> – Mark Labberton,
> President, Fuller Theological Seminary

"Bobby Schuller is a compelling communicator with a passionate faith who teaches the Bible with a refreshing style that makes me want to follow Jesus with greater devotion. *Happiness According to Jesus* unpacks the greatest sermon ever preached with the keen understanding of a professor and the heart and sensitivity of a pastor."

– Gene Appel,
Senior Pastor, Eastside Christian Church, Anaheim, CA

"With humility, practical insight, and wisdom Bobby shares from his heart how all of us can live a wonderful life rooted in the book of Matthew! Not a stranger from the limelight or from pain, Bobby gives us a timely gift of encouragement to live life to the fullest in his book, *Happiness According to Jesus: What It Means to Be Blessed.*"

– Dave Gibbons,
Strategic Advisor and
Founder of NEWSONG.NET and XEALOTS.ORG

"Uplifting, encouraging, and comforting, Bobby Schuller takes us to the mountainside where we hear the Sermon on the Mount like we've never heard it before. Through his explanation of ancient culture blended with modern-day examples, we gain insight and clarity into what is believed by many to be Christ's most beloved and powerful words. *Happiness According to Jesus* is not to be missed."

– Doug Mazza,
President, Joni and Friends International
Disability Center

BOBBY
SCHULLER

HOST OF *HOUR OF POWER*

HAPPINESS
ACCORDING TO
JESUS

WHAT IT MEANS TO
BE BLESSED

WORTHY
PUBLISHING

Copyright © 2015 by Robert V. Schuller

Published by Worthy Books, an imprint of Worthy Publishing Group, a division of Worthy Media, Inc., One Franklin Park, 6100 Tower Circle, Suite 210, Franklin, TN 37067.

WORTHY is a registered trademark of Worthy Media, Inc.

HELPING PEOPLE EXPERIENCE THE HEART OF GOD

eBook available wherever digital books are sold.

Library of Congress Cataloging-in-Publication Data

Schuller, Bobby, 1981-

Happiness according to Jesus : what it means to be blessed / by Robert V. Schuller.
  pages cm

ISBN 978-1-61795-521-1 (tradepaper : alk. paper)

1. Sermon on the mount--Criticism, interpretation, etc. 2. Happiness--Biblical teaching. I. Title. II. Title: What it means to be blessed.

BT380.3.S38 2015

226.9'06--dc23

2015003595

Unless otherwise noted, Scripture quotations are taken from The Holy Bible, New International Version®, NIV® Copyright © 1973, 1978, 1984, 2011 by Biblica, Inc.® Used by permission. All rights reserved worldwide. Scripture quotations marked ESV are taken from The English Standard Version. © 2001 by Crossway Bibles, a division of Good News Publishers.

Italics added to Scripture quotations are the author's emphasis.

For foreign and subsidiary rights, contact rights@worthypublishing.com

Some names and identifying details have been changed to protect the privacy of the individuals involved.

Published in association with Yates & Yates, yates2.com.

Cover Design: Micah Kandros Design, www.micahkandrosdesign.com

Interior Design and Typesetting: Christopher Hudson & Associates, Inc.

Printed in the United States of America
15 16 17 18 19 RRD 8 7 6 5 4 3 2 1

To my friend and mentor Bill Gaultiere, a pastor of pastors.

Contents

Foreword

by John Ortberg

WHY DO WE not more often associate the word *Christian* with the word *happy*?

Thinkers as far back as Aristotle noted that happiness is what everyone is chasing. A preacher friend of mine notes that, for the most part, people are not on a "truth quest"; they're on a "happy quest." Yet when it comes to happiness we tend to think of people with lots of money or fame, or we seek advice from positive psychologists or life coaches or the blogosphere.

What if there was another possibility?

Out of all the books and posts and research and messages that have ever been given on the subject, the single most influential talk on the subject of happiness was—purely as a matter of historical fact—what has come to be known as the Sermon on the Mount.

The first word in this talk—often translated "Blessed," which unfortunately has taken on many religious barnacles— was a pronouncement of who possesses (or can possess) the good life. Who is the fortunate one? Who should we look upon with admiration? Who is in a position to be emulated?

It's the last person you might expect. It's the disappointed. It's the left out. It's the loner, the loser, or the rejected lover.

It could be me.

It could be you.

It's anyone who discovers that God's address is at-the-end-of-my-rope.com.

Happiness is like the horizon: the more we pursue it, the more elusive it becomes. You can't achieve happiness if your main goal is to achieve happiness. Happiness always comes as a by-product of the pursuit of something else, something nobler.

So it's time to sit at the feet of the Master of happiness. He once said to his friends that he was teaching them so that *his* joy could be in *them* and that *their* joy would be running out their ears.

The most joyful man who ever lived was Jesus. It is time, in this happiness-obsessed, joy-challenged world—to go to the Master of the subject.

That is what Bobby Schuller has done.

You cannot read through these pages without realizing that these are the thoughts of one who has savored and absorbed and pondered and wrestled with and lived these words.

For Jesus, like the master of any subject, will say things that are not intuitively obvious:

> *If someone strikes you on the right cheek, turn to them the other cheek also.*

> *If someone forces you to go with them one mile, go with them two.*

If someone sues you to take your shirt, give them your cloak as well.

Give to the one who borrows from you.

Bless those who curse you.

These do not immediately strike us as sound laws for a happy life. And of course, if we take them as laws to be mechanically obeyed, they are not. But as Bobby notes, Jesus is not giving us "a new legalism." Rather, "he's telling us to think of creative, nonhostile ways to resolve things quickly with people who curse us." These are illustrations of what it looks like to live in the reality Jesus calls "the kingdom of the heavens."

"Christians destroy our enemies by making them our friends," Bobby says. What a great way of putting it! It's the greatest enemy-destruction plan of all time, a plan infinitely greater than any army carried out.

It's how God dealt with us when we were not reconciled to him.

I am excited for you to read this book because it is filled with great insights and wonderful wisdom. I'm also excited for you to read this book because it reflects the wisdom of a mentor Bobby and I share: Dallas Willard, who lived in the reality of this message like no one I've ever known. Dallas loved to listen to Bobby teach, and Bobby loved to teach what Dallas knew and lived and experienced and guided so many of us into. Dallas was—because of Jesus—the truly happiest man I have ever known.

But in the end, it's the mentorship of Jesus that matters. We keep misunderstanding him, misapplying him, and misappropriating him. You'd think he might get impatient and look for a better group of followers.

But he is patient as well as joyful. He is somehow content to continue to hand his treasure even to those of us who live it and communicate it so imperfectly.

Then, every once in a while, as a gift of grace, someone sees the treasure, hungers for it afresh, and points to it in a way so that others, too, may run after it.

That is what this book is about.

Read it and grow happy.

Acknowledgments

I WAS JUST FINISHING seminary and everyone was talking about this great book called *Divine Conspiracy* by Dallas Willard. I got about halfway through and just didn't get it. It was long and hard to understand—even boring at times—so the book found its way to a random bookshelf in my office. A couple of years later I began to spend time with one of Dallas's students, Bill Gaultiere. After learning from Bill and seeing how Dallas's understanding of Jesus' teaching impacted Bill, I picked up *Divine Conspiracy* another time. This time it changed my life. My copy of the book is now barely holding together from overuse. I have read all of Dallas's works, listened to endless YouTube videos, and yes, even some cassette tapes of his teaching. I had to meet him.

I got in touch with Dallas via e-mail and he met me at the Catalyst Conference held at Mariners Church in California. He was the warmest and most loving person I have ever met. As he was talking quietly to me about moral knowledge, a band was blasting in the background playing a Britney Spears song. The contrast was amusing if not ironic. From there, Dallas took me under his wing as a brief mentor and dear friend. He would meet with me at his office at USC and take what seemed like all the time in the world for this young pastor and dreamer. Even when he was sick, he and Jane would send encouraging e-mails about my sermons on the *Hour of Power.* His is a life that will forever be treasured.

I am incredibly indebted to the life and work of Dallas Willard, as well as those he influenced—specifically John Ortberg and Bill Gaultiere. John is America's greatest living Christian teacher, and his writing and sermons influenced my life and ministry in too many ways to count. Bill, like John and Dallas, has put on the mind of Christ in a way that is palpable to all who are with him. He has been one of my closest friends and spiritual directors for years.

I also want to thank my teaching team, who gathers every Thursday to help me write my sermons: Chad Blake, Kirstie Weeks, Tully Wilkinson, and Michael Bischof. Their thoughts touch nearly every page of this book.

I'm especially grateful to Byron Williamson and the team at Worthy Publishing for catching the vision for this book.

Finally, I wouldn't be anywhere without my beloved wife, Hannah, and my whole family. Their love and encouragement has made my ministry a reality.

• •

Now when Jesus saw the crowds, he went up on a mountainside and sat down. His disciples came to him, and he began to teach them.

—Matthew 5:1–2

• •

Introduction

A New Day,
A New Person

THE SERMON ON THE MOUNT is my favorite text in the whole Bible. If I were a scholar of any part of the Bible, it would be the Sermon on the Mount. I have spent years reading books on the subject, I've memorized it, I've translated it from Greek to English, I've examined it, I've bounced ideas off it, and it has formed the way I view ministry. In probably four out of every five sermons I give, I touch at least at one point on the Sermon on the Mount. I'll mention loving your enemies or turning the cheek. I'll mention living honestly. I'll mention the Lord's Prayer. I'll mention the Beatitudes. All these things are part of this important message, which is the greatest sermon ever preached. The Sermon on the Mount was preached by Jesus long ago, yet it still abides today as the best way to direct people into Christian living.

Jesus was a rabbi. He was a teacher who wanted his students to go beyond just learning his principles. He wanted his students to live like him. He wanted his students to walk like him and talk like him. He wanted his students to joke like him, eat like him, and treat people around them as he would treat people around him. Rabbis in Jesus' day not only taught principles but wanted to make clones of themselves. That's something we often miss in our Western worldview.

A recent story was told of a student from a prestigious Ivy League school who got an A in ethics and yet was arrested for rape. How does someone who gets an A in ethics become a rapist? In our Western worldview, there's no problem there because getting an A in ethics in a Western university only means that you know principles, not that you believe in them or apply them in any way. Dallas Willard told me that once, at the end of his ethics class, he asked his students, "How many of you understand ethics now?" All of them raised their hands. Then he said, "How many of you tend to be ethical?" The students laughed because in our world, we believe if we can just learn certain principles, that's enough. But it's not. Jesus wanted his students to be like him, act like him, walk like him, and talk like him. So he gave the Sermon on the Mount as a vision of what it would look like to live this kind of life.

Jesus wanted obedient apprentices. When we look at the Great Commission, we often think Jesus said, "Go out and preach the gospel." But he didn't say that. He said, "Go and make disciples of all nations, baptizing them in the name of the Father and of the Son and of the Holy Spirit, and teaching them to obey everything I have commanded you" (Matthew 28:19–20). It's very different. Jesus commands his disciples to go out and make disciples, make students, make apprentices of his way of life.

Jesus' Invitation to Life

The Sermon on the Mount is Jesus giving a vision of his life. Imagine droves of people following him. They are following him because he's a great healer! He's raising the dead and healing the sick, and amazing things are happening. So, of course, they want to hear what he's going to say.

He's standing by the shoreline and thousands of people go up and sit on a hill so they can all hear him. It's a warm day, and the Sea of Galilee is behind him. He gives them the most wonderful gift that has ever been given to humanity—this discourse. It's his vision of what it's like to live in the kingdom of God. And then he tells them that if they obey these words, they are like a man or a woman whose life is built on the foundation of a rock. And if they don't obey these words, then they become like a fool who builds his house on sand.

And this is where we get lost because, when we look at the Sermon on the Mount, we see a way of living that is difficult. We look at these things Jesus commands us to do and we think that it's impossible. Some of us even say that it's offensive. We think it is too hard. We're lost because we think, *Obeying what Jesus says in the Sermon on the Mount means doing what I don't want to do even though it's the right thing to do.*

That's not what the Sermon on the Mount is. The Sermon on the Mount is an invitation to a life that's better than anything we can put together on our own. It's an invitation to give up being an angry person and to become a person of peace. It's an invitation to stop wearing masks. It's an invitation to stop lying and no longer be burdened by constantly trying to remember things and patching up things with people when they lose trust in you. It's an invitation to live the kind of life where you can smile because it's not your job to judge people; it's not your job to tell it like it is. It's a life in which you don't have to worry. It's a life in which money doesn't matter as much as you think it does. The kind of life Jesus invites us to in the Sermon on the Mount is eternal life. It is a great gift, yet so many people are offended when they read these words.

A Divine Dichotomy

Not long ago, a professor at Texas A&M presented the Sermon on the Mount and asked her students to write an essay.[1] Many of these students said, "It's offensive!" "It's impossible!" "What? You mean if I just look at a woman, I'm committing adultery?" "If somebody slaps me on the face I'm just supposed to take it?" See, there's this confusion that "I can't do that." "I don't want to do that." "That's not fair." "This is archaic." "This is stupid."

It has been said that any Christian who read the Sermon on the Mount all the way through would fall on his knees and say, "Lord, save me from the Sermon on the Mount!" We want others to follow the Sermon the Mount. We would love for other people to do what Jesus is talking about in the Sermon on the Mount. How great would it be to live in a world where nobody judged you, nobody pressed you or pushed you, and nobody ever got angry with you? We think, *If everybody except me did that, things would be great.*

The Sermon on the Mount is an invitation to a wonderful life. But Jesus says sometimes it's an easy yoke, and then other times it's a narrow and difficult road. Well, which is it? Is it easy or is it difficult?

The best way to understand this dichotomy, I think, is a story. Years ago, I knew a girl who worked at Blockbuster, and she was brilliant. She got top scores on the SAT and the ACT tests. So she decided to go for it: she applied to Harvard. And you know what? She got in. She even got a full-ride scholarship. This girl working at Blockbuster had an opportunity to go to the most prestigious university in the world—but she didn't. I remember walking into Blockbuster one day and she was still there. I asked, "When are you going to Harvard?" And she surprised me by saying she decided not to go. I said, "You're not going?" Why wouldn't she go?

We have all sorts of theories. She loved working at Blockbuster, perhaps. Limitless amount of rentals; that's something. I imagine going to Harvard seemed scary. I imagine she had a low self-esteem. I imagine that the work seemed daunting. I imagine that at Harvard there would be incredible expectations put on her that she didn't feel like she could fulfill. A life at Harvard probably seemed too difficult compared to a life at Blockbuster. And so she just continued to work at Blockbuster. When I left Oklahoma, that was the last time I ever saw her. Blockbuster is out of business now, by the way. I wonder what she's doing.

When you look at the Sermon on the Mount and think, *This life is too hard for me; I can't live that way*, you are like this girl at Blockbuster who didn't take her free ride to Harvard. Yes, going to Harvard is a ton of work! You're going to be studying all the time, pulling all-nighters, and eating Ramen noodles and drinking recycled coffee. College is hard. But imagine how different her life would be if she would have done it.

That's how the calling to be a Jesus kind of person is. It's difficult. It's letting people hurt you more than you think is fair. It's abandoning the attention and acclaim of others to live in God's love, which can feel distant. It's ridding your life of many pleasurable idols, shattering your beloved gods, eating crow, serving the outcasts, radical truth-telling, and secret goodness. It's all sorts of difficult things, but it is like going to Harvard—it is the greatest opportunity to live in the fullest, richest, most exciting life you could possibly have.

The general theme of the Sermon on the Mount is this: "It's God's plan to overcome evil with good in human history and to use each one of us to do it."[2] That quote is from Dallas Willard, who has given to us the most wonderful gift ever— pure, spiritual knowledge about how to live in God's reality.

Let me ask you: how's your life now? For those of you who have rejected the teachings of Jesus, how's it going? Do you feel like you have it together? Do you have a strength that can't be broken? Do you feel like a palm tree in the wind that bends but always stands and becomes stronger? Or do you feel like you're flying upside down? Do you feel lost? Looking back, how many times has screaming at someone, hoarding money, or lying ever helped you? How's your life now, for those of you who have rejected the kingdom way of life? The Sermon on the Mount is an invitation to something wonderful.

The Parable of the Cave

One of the best ways to understand what Jesus is doing through the Sermon on the Mount is Plato's parable of the cave. Plato was a great philosopher who studied under Socrates, and he wanted to talk about wisdom. So his parable of the cave goes something like this.

Imagine there's a short wall inside a dark and damp cave. Along this wall several people are sitting on the ground. They're chained to one wall and staring at another wall at the end of the cave. Behind them is light from the fires that are burning. There is also pottery behind them, but they can't see that because their backs are against the wall.

Does this make sense yet? Visualize the fire shining light against those pots and making shadows on the wall. So the people chained inside the cave think those shadows flickering on the wall are reality. In this bizarre story, they've always been chained to this wall from the beginning of their existence. They've never seen anything else except those shadows. So they think that's what's real.

One day, a man looks down and his shackles are open. He's free! As he gets up, it hurts. Then he turns around and sees something behind him and it's earth-shattering. There are pots, and a flame, which he's never seen before. And then he starts to put two and two together. He sees the flame behind the pots, and he sees the shadows, and he realizes those shadows aren't what he thought they were. Their image wasn't real. What is real is this flame.

Then he looks down, sees a pinpoint of light way at the end of the cave, and starts walking toward it. As he gets closer, he starts running to the point of light. As the cave starts to open up and he gets closer to the light, he steps outside and sees the mountains, the sky, the ocean, and the trees. He thinks, *Wow, this is the most amazing thing I've ever seen!* Then he remembers his friends who are still chained to that wall, and he wants to tell them about this whole world they don't know even exists. They don't know what blue looks like. They don't know what fresh air smells like.

So the man runs back into the cave. Now what happens when you've been outside in the sun on a bright summer day and then you go into a dark place? You can't see anything, right? So he comes in and finds his friends, but he's nearly blind because his eyes haven't adjusted to the darkness of the cave. He's tripping and knocking over things, trying to tell his friends about this amazing place that he doesn't have words to describe. He doesn't have a word for *river* or *mountain* or *sky*, so he's using his limited language to try to explain this incredible world out there, and he sounds like a buffoon. He's blind, he's knocking things over, and his friends who are chained on the wall begin laughing at him and mocking him as a crazy person.

That's the end of the parable—a parable about knowledge and wisdom.

This is the kind of thing that Jesus is doing in the Sermon on the Mount. He is coming to people who are chained on a wall, and he is inviting them to exit the cave with him. And as he's doing this, people are mocking him, people are saying he is possessed by demons, and people are saying he is crazy. Some people believe him, but other people don't. Some walk out of the cave and others stay.

This kind of life is in such great contrast to the world around us. It's a life that, when you model it for people, they will look at you and think, *I'm so glad he lives that way. It makes me want to be around him.* Yet they also think, *But I don't want to be like that.* And that's the trap.

The teachings of Jesus invite us to Harvard. They invite us to exit the cave. They invite us into a new reality where the process is difficult but the life is so rich, so full, and so aflame that you know you can't die. Do you have that knowledge? Are you so full of the life of God that you say, "I am living eternally right now and I know I will never taste death"? That's the kind of life that Jesus is talking about in the Sermon on the Mount.

You can trust Jesus. You can trust what he is about to teach us in the Sermon on the Mount.

If you believe this and dedicate your life to live out what Jesus preached in the Sermon on the Mount, then incredible revival will break out in your life and community like you have never seen. But it means trusting Jesus. It's not easy to love your enemies. It's not easy to always tell the truth. The life Jesus calls us to is difficult, but we can trust him.

Words of Life

So the Sermon on the Mount sounds something like this: All of you who are suffering, rejoice because the kingdom of God is here. You are the ones God has called to change the world. God has given the Scripture, he has given the prophets, and now this sermon from Jesus will guide us. And if we read it carefully, we will see something like this:

- Don't be angry. Give anger to the Lord.
- Settle matters quickly with people who are against you.
- Don't ever lie. It's too much to remember.
- Don't swear.
- Don't pound your fist.
- Live an honest life.
- When people harm you, bless them.
- When people gossip about you, say good things about them.
- When people get everything about you wrong, thank the Lord, because that's what people did to the great prophets of the world.
- When you give to the needy or those who need help, do it as secretly as possible.
- Never do good or righteous things for the acclaim of man, but do it for the acclaim and the glory of God.
- When you pray, pray simply. Don't show off to people.
- When you fast, don't let anybody know.

- Don't dedicate your life to storing up all sorts of material wealth. Money is used for the sake of bettering the world.
- Don't worry about what you're going to wear; don't worry about what you're going to eat; don't worry about anything. You have nothing to worry about because you are an eternal being in God's great universe. And this Creator loves you. You have nothing to worry about.
- Don't judge people.
- Don't shove religion down people's throats.
- If you need something from God and you know him, just ask him, and the door will be opened.
- Love those who hate you, bless those who curse you, and you will be made a whole person.

Take these words and live them out, and you will flourish in God's wonderful kingdom.

• •

Blessed are the poor in spirit,
  for theirs is the kingdom of heaven.
Blessed are those who mourn,
  for they will be comforted.
Blessed are the meek,
  for they will inherit the earth.
Blessed are those who hunger and thirst for
righteousness,
  for they will be filled.
Blessed are the merciful,
  for they will be shown mercy.
Blessed are the pure in heart,
  for they will see God.
Blessed are the peacemakers,
  for they will be called children of God.
Blessed are those who are persecuted because of
righteousness,
  for theirs is the kingdom of heaven.

  Blessed are you when people insult you,
persecute you and falsely say all kinds of evil
against you because of me. Rejoice and be glad,
because great is your reward in heaven, for in
the same way they persecuted the prophets who
were before you.

—Matthew 5:3–12

• •

1 Happiness and Suffering

THE SERMON ON THE MOUNT begins with the famous Beatitudes. Here Jesus is addressing, essentially, the issue of suffering.

Last year, my then two-year-old son, Cohen, started having seizures. One particular episode almost took his life. My wife wrote in her journal:

> I was exhausted as I drove home from the hospital today. My mind was unable to focus on anything except the image of Cohen lying lifeless in the ambulance. I really thought he was gone. My body felt crushed in; I couldn't breathe. But he's alive and with no brain damage; thank you, Jesus. Thank you!
>
> As I drove home, a car in front of me had an advertisement decaled over the entire back of the car. It was some type of ad about

running for charity. The main photo was a picture of a little boy and beneath his photo it said, "In loving memory of Chase." I burst into tears. I couldn't stop weeping the whole way home. A mother had lost her son when he was so young. I kept saying to myself through my tears, "There's *so* much suffering in this world. There's so much suffering."

After countless hours in the hospital, the doctors discovered Cohen has a slight brain malformation that causes brain waves to misfire, which causes seizures. He is three years old now and I'm happy to say we've seen a lot of improvement. Nothing can describe the suffering that Hannah and I went through last year as we feared for our son's health and life.

The Problem of Suffering

Many of us are suffering. Some of us have lost a loved one, have lost a job, have little money, or have received a bad health report. If you are suffering, Jesus says you are blessed because the kingdom of God is made available to you. There are few things in this world that prohibit people from believing in God, loving God, or getting close to God more than suffering.

Suffering is the number one way the enemy tries to convince people to doubt God. The enemy knows the ultimate suffering humankind cannot endure is the void in the pit of the soul that can only be filled with God's love and goodness. The enemy knows that if he can cause you to doubt God and then be separated from God because of suffering, he's won.

There are all sorts of ways we can address suffering philosophically. We can talk about the issue of choice—that without suffering, there's no choice. Without choice, there is no love. Without choice, there is no meaning. My favorite example of this is the *Bruce Almighty* defense. In the movie *Bruce Almighty,* the title character (played by Jim Carrey) is mad at God, so God decides to allow Bruce to be God for a day. And everything goes horribly wrong. Bruce gets all these voices in his head, prayer requests from everybody praying, and he's going crazy. So he says he wants all prayer requests in letter form. Instantly the room fills up with letters. Wanting something smaller, he changes his mind and says he wants all requests on Post-It notes, and he's covered in Post-It notes. Finally he says that he wants them in e-mails. His computer fills up with millions of e-mails.

He starts to read one e-mail after another. It's too much to handle, so he decides to answer yes to every prayer request. That's when things really get bad. First, everyone wins the lottery. But because thousands of people win the lottery, the winnings are split and everybody only gets about twenty dollars.

If we are human beings then we hate suffering. When a kid dies, that's a horrible thing. There's a part of us that says pain is bad, guilt is bad, and loneliness is bad. That part of us is the godly part. The very fact that you hate suffering is one of the absolute proofs of God. Suffering is against the heart of God. God hates suffering, he wants to overcome it, and he wants to use people to do it.

This is how Jesus begins the Sermon on the Mount. Jesus is at the beginning of his ministry. He kicks it off by healing a bunch of people. All the rest of these people, many of whom are also sick and hurting, want to follow him because they're hoping he'll heal them. He's become famous for all the miracles he's performed. There he is, standing on a mountain and thousands of people are gathered. They're not an audience but a line of people who want to get healed. Some of these people have leprosy. Some are bleeding. Some are dying. Some have no money. Some are hungry. And they're waiting in line for Jesus to bless them. For these people, to be blessed means "I will be fed," and to be blessed means "I will be cured," and to be blessed means "I will have money." Jesus is going to heal these people. We see him doing that at the end of the story. However, before he heals them physically, he wants to give them knowledge of what it means to be blessed.

The word translated "blessed" here is *makarios*, which means to be happy, to be filled with joy and a flourishing life. These people think a flourishing life means money and health, and Jesus begins his Sermon on the Mount by disagreeing with them. In his day, society considered the most blessed people to be the Roman elite or the Pharisees. The Roman elite believed in power and wealth, prestige and glory. Some of the people listening to Jesus that day thought, *If could be like the Romans with power, prestige, money, and glory, then I will be blessed.* The Pharisees taught that the one who is blessed is the one who follows the law perfectly. For example, they didn't believe you could spit on the ground on the Sabbath because if the spit rolled and collected dirt, then it would be considered "work." The Pharisees touted a hefty, soul-killing legalism. So some of the people listening to Jesus believed, *If I could be like the Pharisees—if I could be holy enough, be super religious, and follow the law perfectly—then I will be blessed.*

These people presumed to know what it meant to be blessed. So Jesus begins his sermon by essentially telling them that's not what it means to be blessed. Being blessed is not about power, and it's not about legalism. It's not about glory, money, romance, or fame. What is it about? Jesus will tell us, beginning with the Beatitudes.

The Beatitudes

There are two schools of thought about the Beatitudes. Most people teach that the Beatitudes are a way to live your life. For example, you should be "poor in spirit." You should "mourn." You should be "meek." You should "hunger and thirst for righteousness." This is one school of thought, and there is a lot of good that can come out of a study like that. It's usually a good thing because usually the way the study goes is "poor in spirit" means humble, or something like that. "Meek" means you don't push or insist on your own way. Those are good things to do, they really are. However, I'm from a different school that believes what Jesus is doing in the Beatitudes is not giving eight new commandments about how to live life. He's not giving eight new attitudes for powerful living. He's simply making a declaration to people who are suffering.

The first Beatitude is, "Blessed are the poor in spirit" (Matthew 5:3). "Poor in spirit" means to be spiritually bankrupt. It means to have very little moral or biblical or religious knowledge. Jesus says, "Theirs is the kingdom of heaven." If you don't know anything about God or the Bible, if you have never been religious, then good news! The kingdom of God is just for you.

"Blessed are those who mourn" (v. 4). To mourn is to be totally overcome with sadness and pain at the loss of someone you loved and not having any idea how to cope with it. If you are in mourning, then good news! You will find incredible comfort in the kingdom of God, your home.

"Blessed are the meek" (v. 5). The "meek" are people who don't stand up or speak up for themselves, people who are overrun, the doormats. Jesus says they'll inherit the earth. If you are always pushed around, then good news! In the kingdom of God the weak will be made strong.

"Blessed are those who hunger and thirst for righteousness" (v. 6). That word "righteousness" is the Greek word *dikaiosyne*, which means justice. Blessed are those who "hunger and thirst" for justice in their lives. It's the father whose daughter was violated and the guy was never caught. It's the mother whose son was murdered and the murderer was never brought to justice. If you hunger and thirst for justice, then good news! Justice will reign in the city of God!

Jesus is speaking to people who are overcome with incredible sadness and suffering. And he says, blessed are you in the midst of your terrible suffering, in the midst of your horrible circumstances, because the kingdom of God has arrived. Jesus is saying, "I have come in the midst of your terrible cries to God to bring hope and life, renewal and joy." Jesus is not saying you are blessed when you are poor in spirit; he's saying you are blessed in spite of being poor in spirit. A new day has come. He's not saying you are blessed because you mourn; he's saying you are blessed in spite of the fact that you're in terrible mourning—because the kingdom of God has come. Things are going to be made new.

In Luke 6:20–22, it's clearer that Jesus is talking about suffering people, not a new list of moral imperatives. Jesus says, "Blessed are you who are poor . . . Blessed are you who hunger now . . . Blessed are you who weep now . . . Blessed are you when people hate you, when they exclude you and insult you." Jesus is speaking to people who are suffering. He's talking to people who had been beat up by religion, people who were starving, people who were sick, people who had no hope. He's saying to them, "You are blessed."

My friend Dr. Bill Gaultiere paraphrases the Sermon on the Mount like this:

> Blessed are you when you're spiritually poor for you can live in the kingdom of the heavens.
>
> Blessed are you if you're grieving a loss for you can experience God's comfort.
>
> Blessed are you if you're shy for you can inherit the best the earth has to offer.
>
> Blessed are you if you're suffering from injustice for you can be filled with God's life.
>
> Blessed are you if you're tenderhearted toward all who are wounded and needy for you know God's tender heart for you.
>
> Blessed are you if you're pursuing seemingly unattainable ideals, for you can find God.

Blessed are you if you keep getting caught in the middle of conflicts for you can be at peace as God's child.

Blessed are you if you're persecuted badly for you can live in the kingdom of the heavens where there is a reason to jump for joy.

Who Is Blessed Today?

In Jesus' day, people had the same misconceptions about happiness that we do today. Who is blessed today? If you were to go around and read people's minds to get the honest answer to the question, "Who do you think is the most blessed today?" you would see, based on the way people live their lives, who they think is truly blessed. People essentially say that those who are famous, those who are healthy, and those who have lots of money are blessed. They couldn't be further from the truth.

Think about the way you live your own life. Do you live for these material things more than anything else? If so, you believe these are the things that make a person blessed. I hope you are healthy. I hope you are rich. Keep in mind I do not think it's bad to be rich, and I do not think it's bad to be healthy. Nevertheless, I hope you know it has little to do with the thriving, fulfilling, life-giving kingdom of God, which is available to everyone. We will all leave the world as naked as we came. What of our lives then?

All of us suffer. All of us have pain. All of us have guilt. All of us constantly go through change. All of us suffer loneliness. Jesus comes onto the scene to say to you and to say to me that there is hope, and that hope is in Jesus. There is this deep hole within every human being that can only be filled by God. If that hole remains empty, we deceive ourselves by thinking it can be filled with anything else. Jesus is teaching his people that filling that void, that hole, with his life leads to the greatest, most fulfilling, most exciting life ever.

Jesus is saying in the Beatitudes that even if you're suffering, you're blessed if you have him. Even if you're suffering, there is hope—you will overcome. Even if you are broken, even if you are sick, even if you've lost everything, there is hope. You don't need to give up. Jesus is saying, "You have a wonderful present—a wonderful today—in me because I am here. And you have a wonderful future if your future has me in it." This is what Jesus is teaching in the Sermon on the Mount. No matter how bad our suffering gets in life, if we have Jesus, we can get through anything.

The Message of the Beatitudes

The message of the Beatitudes is this: Even if you're poor in spirit, you have hope because Jesus has you in his hands. If you're in mourning, if you're meek, if you're humble, if you're persecuted, if people hate you, if people say bad things about you, then you have the unending favor, life, and love of God. And no one can take that from you. No matter how sick you are, no matter if you've been told you have a week to live, you have hope and a wonderful future with Jesus. No matter how run-down, poor, or broken you are, if you have Christ in your life, then you have a bright future. And you can trust him.

● ●

You are the salt of the earth. But if the salt loses its saltiness, how can it be made salty again? It is no longer good for anything, except to be thrown out and trampled underfoot.

You are the light of the world. A town built on a hill cannot be hidden. Neither do people light a lamp and put it under a bowl. Instead they put it on its stand, and it gives light to everyone in the house. In the same way, let your light shine before others, that they may see your good deeds and glorify your Father in heaven.

—Matthew 5:13–16

● ●

2 Salty Do-Gooders

GEORGE SAUNDERS, BELOVED short story writer, essayist, and professor, gave the convocation speech at a Syracuse University graduation ceremony.[1] He began by saying that a traditional form for graduation speeches has become, "Some old fart, his best years behind him . . . gives heartfelt advice to a group of shining, energetic young people, with all of their best years ahead of them." He said one of the best questions you can ask an old person is, "Looking back, what do you regret?"

Saunders said when he looked back on his life he didn't regret the horrible jobs he had, like being a "knuckle puller in a slaughterhouse." He didn't regret being poor from time to time. He didn't even regret swimming in a river in the Sumatra naked, a little buzzed, only to look up and see three hundred monkeys sitting above the river, pooping into the water that he was swimming in, and being sick for seven months afterward. He didn't even regret embarrassing himself by falling at a hockey game and flinging his hockey stick at a girl he liked.

Saunders continued that something he did regret happened in seventh grade, with a girl named Ellen. She had "blue cat's-eye glasses that, at the time, only old ladies wore." She chewed on her hair. She was very quiet and people loved to pick on her and put her in her place. She tried every day to just disappear and be left alone. Saunders imagined that she would go home and her mom would ask her, "Ellen, how was your day today, sweetie?" And she would say, "Oh, fine." When in fact things were terrible, and she felt like nobody loved her, and she just wanted to disappear. Then one day, Ellen's family moved away. What Saunders regretted is that he never had the courage to be kind to Ellen. He said what he regrets most in life are "failures of kindness." He didn't pick on Ellen, he didn't contribute to the nasty things that people were saying to her, but she never had a person in that school who loved her or cared for her. Now, some forty-odd years later, that's what he regrets.

I believe that George Saunders regrets he wasn't kind to that girl because George Saunders, like you, was designed to be a kind person. You were made by God to be salt and to be light (Matthew 5:13–16). And the further you, as a human being, veer from God's intent for you to be salt and light—the further you go into your own wickedness, selfishness, and anger—the further you move away from being the person God intended you to be, which includes things like being kind to this girl in seventh grade. You become, in a way, less human.

24

The less illuminating, the less salty you are, the less human you are in the sense that you're much less than what God intended for you to be.

In Matthew 5 Jesus is speaking to a large group of people, most of whom are suffering. They think to be blessed means to have lots of money and health, or to be super religious and get everything right. Yet Jesus tells them plainly that's not what it means to be blessed. To be blessed means to be a part of God's kingdom. He says to these intensely suffering people, "You're blessed because you have me, Jesus. I have come here for you. And as a king ushers in a new reign, I am now ushering in God's reign."

You Are Salt

Then Jesus says . . . to these people that they, not the Pharisees or Roman elite, are salt and light.

Jesus says, looking at these people, "You are the salt of the earth. But if the salt loses its saltiness, how can it be made salty again? It is no longer good for anything, except to be thrown out and trampled underfoot. You are the light of the world. A town built on a hill cannot be hidden. Neither do people light a lamp and put it under a bowl. Instead they put it on its stand, and it gives light to everyone in the house. In the same way, let your light shine before others, that they may see your good deeds and glorify your Father in heaven" (Matthew 5:13–16).

Now, to first-century Jewish ears, this would have been a startling statement—especially since he said it to regular people. You might have expected Jesus to say something this flattering to a famous rabbi or to a great leader. However, to say this to blue-collar, hurting folk—to say to regular people, "You are the salt of the earth" and "You are the light of the world"—was culturally shocking.

Salt in Jesus' day was very precious. We don't understand that anymore because we have fridges. Today you buy meat or vegetables or fruit, and you want it to last, so you stick it in the fridge. Refrigerators are a relatively new invention that made salt simply a spice. However, throughout history salt was used to pickle and preserve food. You'd use salt on your meat. Some of you are old enough to remember what it was like not having a refrigerator. You probably salted your meats or pickled your vegetables. My grandma told me that when they didn't have a fridge she used to dig a hole in the ground, put some ice in there, and that's where they would store their perishables.

So in a day when there's no refrigeration and you can't just make ice, salt was super valuable and it was used by everybody. Salt was so valuable that it's where we get the word *salary*. The Latin word for salt is *sal*. *Salary* is what the Romans used to pay their soldiers, and it comes from a payment of salt. *Salad* also came from salted vegetables.

So salt was a very precious, valuable thing in Jesus' day, used to clean and preserve food. You'd feel comfort back in the day when you ate something salty because likely it was clean.

Most importantly, salt is delicious. It's just so good. Salt has flavor, and that was true back then as it is today. In Jesus' day, only an emperor would be able to take a bowl of salt and sprinkle it liberally on his food. Back then, salt was so precious that they would dilute it in a sauce to extend its use. The idea of sprinkling salt on my hamburger or fries in Jesus' day would have been incredible, like sprinkling money on my food to make it taste better.

I like salt. I like salt so much that when I go to a Mexican restaurant with my friends, I don't ask if I can put salt on the chips; I ask if I can put chips on the salt. If you've ever wondered why bacon is so good, it's because it's salty. If you want to make something that's sweet even better, add some salt to it. Seriously. Think about what is salty-sweet in this world: kettle corn, toffee, caramel, margaritas, In-N-Out shakes.

Jesus wants us to be disciples who have flavor and life, and who make life better for those around us. Everybody usually wants more salt. Yet how many people want more Christians in their life? It depends on what your experience has been. Some of you would say you don't want any more Christians. Many people, when they think of Christians, don't think of flavorful, salty, alive people. Oliver Wendell Holmes said, "I might have entered the Christian ministry if certain clergymen I knew had not looked and acted so much like undertakers."[2] Robert Louis Stevenson said he was so happy because, "I have been to church today and I am not depressed!"[3]

Now there's something about a person being salt in a pure and good way that makes this person delicious to life. When you are around a "salty" person, your day and your life are going to be better. We need saltier disciples.

So Jesus is saying to his listeners, "You are valuable, purifying people who give flavor to life." Notice that Jesus does not say, "Once you *were* the salt of the earth." He doesn't even say, "If you follow me and do everything I tell you to do, then you *will become* salty." What does he say? "You *are* the salt of the earth." Jesus is speaking this over people who don't even realize how salty they are. He's saying to be yourself— be your salty self. He's like Rafiki going to Simba and saying, "You're a lion." He's like Morpheus going to Neo and saying, "You're the one."

Jesus is going to people who are already salt, trying to get them to realize who they truly are, saying, "You are salt. Be who you are. Don't lose your saltiness."

You Are Light

Then Jesus says this again another way. He says, "You are the light of the world" (Matthew 5:14). Now this statement would be shocking for some scholars. Most of the time, when Jesus talks about the light of the world, he is talking about himself. Yet notice Jesus doesn't say here, "*I* am the light of the world." In this passage, he says, "*You* are the light of the world." Again, Jesus does not say that you once *were* the light of the world, or that if you try harder you *will become* the light of the world. He says clearly, "This is who you *are*. You are light."

Then he tells his listeners not to hide their light under a bowl. In Jesus' day, they had little clay lamps they used for light, and one lamp was always lit. Why did they do that? Because there were no matches. It was a pain to light a lamp because they had to take out a flint, strike it against something until it sparked, and then catch the sparks on something flammable. That process took a long time. So people would leave one lamp lit and cover it with an earthen bowl, vessel, or bushel with holes in it so that if a leaf or cloth fell on the lamp, it wouldn't burn the house to the ground. That one lamp would stay lit.

The bushel they put over the lit lamp would make the house dark, even though the lamp was still burning. When they got home and removed the bushel, it would be like turning on a light switch. They just pulled the bowl off the top of the lamp, set it aside, and then *boom!*, the whole room lit up. This is what Jesus is saying. He says, "As the light of the world, you are already burning. You are already lit, but you are like a light that has a bushel over the top of it. Take the bushel off!"

Jesus is telling us what a human being actually is. He is saying we are made to be salty, we are made to be light, and when we are anything different or act in a different way, we lose what it means to be a human being. He's telling us, "Shine. Be salty." Jesus says to his people, "Let your light shine before others, that they may see your good deeds and glorify your Father in heaven" (Matthew 5:16).

Be a Salty Do-Gooder

The greatest way you can glorify God, to bring glory to God and save the name of Christianity, is by being a salty do-gooder. That's what he's asking you to be: a salty, flavor-filled, life-giving, happy do-gooder. That's what you, my friends, were made to be. And the further you get from being a salty do-gooder, the further you get from being truly human.

The people listening to Jesus give the Sermon on the Mount were used to the phrase "the light of the world." A famous rabbi, for example, might be considered a light of the world. They said Jerusalem was a light to the Gentiles. But to these very regular, hurting, suffering, aging, dying folk, Jesus says, "You are the light of world. You're the salt of the earth." And what he is really saying to them is, "You're my plan. I have one plan to save the world, and you're it. I've got a plan A, and there's no plan B or plan C. I have one plan and it's you. I intend to overcome evil with good in human history and I intend to use you to do it."

This is going to be a weird metaphor, but imagine I am a lightbulb, an actual Bobby lightbulb, and I'm in a dark room and I decide I want to illuminate this room. I somehow turn myself on. *Boom!* I turn on because my intent is to fill the room with light. I have also illuminated myself. Does that make sense? That is an important part of understanding what it means to be a light and to be salt: when you focus on others, doing good for others, you also become illuminated.

I realized this once with a girl I met at a party. She was the first person I ever led to faith. I did it just by talking to her. I didn't intend to lead her to faith; it just happened. I had just recently devoted my life to Christ when I went to this high school party. There was all sorts of stuff there you don't want to be around, and I had just become a Christian. I said, "I'm not doing this stuff anymore. I'm not going to these parties anymore." Then I felt like God was saying, *Don't run away. Be a light to that world!* So I went, deciding to go in the spirit of listening to God, doing what I felt he was leading me to do. I ended up talking to this girl who was suffering. Her boyfriend was beating her up, she was really into the occult, and she was cutting herself and addicted to drugs. Her dad had vanished, and she was really hurting. For about three hours I talked to her about God's love, his calling on her life, forgiveness of sins, and the joy that comes from being in faith. At the end, she said, "I want that."

So I prayed with her and she received Christ. That moment totally changed her life, and it changed my life too. When I look back at that, the thing I remember most was how I walked away from that conversation feeling so alive. I was used by God to help someone get out of a dark and horrible situation. When I allowed my light to illuminate her life, it also illuminated my darkness. I took the bushel off. I was salty. It was an incredible feeling and it was glorifying to God.

This is Jesus' message: It's not that you will become salty, it's not that you will be a light of the world someday if you try hard enough, but rather you *are* salt. You *are* light. And anything that veers from that veers from what it truly means to be you.

Be Creative in Doing Good

That thing that veers from what God created you to be is called sin. Sin is the selfishness, the anger, the jealousy, the gossip, the bitterness—all the stuff that takes away from your saltiness and your lightness.

God calls us to live our lives in salty, full, and flavorful ways for the benefit of our neighbors—and even our enemies! Believe it or not, we also have to love our enemies. And the way that God calls us to be salt and light is unique to each one of us. We have to be creative.

I have a friend who did the coolest thing. He was doing an outreach to a nursing home, and there were all these sick and elderly people who didn't get to leave the nursing home very often. So he created a prayer team with a group of Christians who were living there. Twice a week he would get together in a room with these nursing home residents and he would bring an armful of prayer requests from suffering people. This group in the nursing home would take hours to pray and intercede for hurting people around the world. That was creative and a unique way to enable those people to continue to contribute to the work of God on earth today. That was the way the young man was able to bless those people, who in turn blessed others.

There are so many things you can do, from caring for the homeless, to giving gifts of charity, or helping your neighbor, to praying for others, or mentoring. If you're a mom or a dad with little kids, that's a mission. We all must remember, "I am light. I am salt. I should not veer from this. This is who God made me to be." All we need to do is simply ask God, "Today I want to be salt and light, what you created me to be. Lord, show me how I can be salt and light to the world around me. How can I be a salty do-gooder in the world?" And you watch, as you lead your life, God will open the doors for you. There's a lot of pain and suffering, but God will use you, if you let him, to bring empathy, hope, vision, and healing.

Finally, don't be overwhelmed thinking you have to save the world by yourself. We're all going to do this together— save the world, I mean. We are. We're going to do it together as a team. Mother Teresa said, "If you can't feed a hundred people, then feed just one."[4] That's a good note to end on because it's not about fixing everything and everyone, burning yourself out, and breaking every boundary. It means just being a salty do-gooder in that fifteen feet of space around you. Sometimes it means just one person or two people God is calling you to reach. If you cannot feed the whole world, just feed one person. Just start there.

Do not think that I have come to abolish the Law or the Prophets; I have not come to abolish them but to fulfill them. For truly I tell you, until heaven and earth disappear, not the smallest letter, not the least stroke of a pen, will by any means disappear from the Law until everything is accomplished. Therefore anyone who sets aside one of the least of these commands and teaches others accordingly will be called least in the kingdom of heaven, but whoever practices and teaches these commands will be called great in the kingdom of heaven. For I tell you that unless your righteousness surpasses that of the Pharisees and the teachers of the law, you will certainly not enter the kingdom of heaven.

—Matthew 5:17–20

3 The Rabbi's Yoke

RECENTLY, BEFORE GIVING a message on the soul-killing nature of legalism, I formed a paper airplane and threw it into my congregation from the pulpit. It was a sheet of paper I had just used to read a deep and meaningful testimony from a Christian who was in prison for her faith. As I finished reading her testimony, I took this sheet and began folding the edges. I was very quiet as I worked. Finally I held the paper airplane in my hand and showed it to the congregation. People started clapping, rooting for me to throw this thing into the air. It launched and did loops, and most people cheered. Others had sour looks on their faces. One guy left.

The main reason I threw a paper airplane is that it's fun. The second reason I threw a paper airplane is that there are many people in the church who don't know fun is sacred.

Legalism and Scripture

In the Sermon on the Mount Jesus has something to say about legalism and Scripture. Legalism has power that, if used wrongly, can make its readers into heartless, religious monsters. In Jesus' day a group of Scripture teachers called Pharisees often used the Bible as a weapon, not against spiritual powers but against hurting people. Today, it's pastors like me who often do this. People use religious traditions or the Bible to hurt and harm and oppress people. If you have been hurt by mean people with Bibles in their hands, I encourage you not to give up on the Bible. Maybe you grew up with parents, or experienced a spouse, a church, or an environment where you've been harmed by the misuse of Scripture. This may have affected your emotions, making you a more anxious or angry or judgmental person. Scripture is not intended to do that to people.

My mom grew up in a very loving but strict church. I remember a story she told about when she was a little girl, walking home from school. She stopped when she saw through a window some little girls doing ballet. She realized at that moment that she could never be a ballerina because, at her church, people weren't allowed to dance.

My mom loved records; she has always loved music. Do you know the song "It's Your Thing," by the Isley Brothers? "It's your thing. Do what you wanna do." My grandma thought it was "Itch your thing." She heard, "Itch your thing," as she was walking past in the hallway and came in, took the record off Mom's record player, and broke it. My mom cried and there was a big emotional mess.

I was talking about this with my grandma (who is one of the sweetest, most godly, incredible women you'd ever meet). She said, "You know, back then it was just so different." This kind of thing was normal for Christians in the 1950s. It was a time when faith was extremely strict and many felt like God was angry constantly. Yet I wonder today if we have simply replaced restrictions against dancing, makeup, and movies for new legalisms that are more fashionable in our faith. Legalism, silly rules, and soul-killing religiosity still plague the church today.

A True View of Righteousness

St. Augustine once said, "Love God and do whatever you please." Now, many people think St. Augustine meant that if you just simply love God, then you can go sin and do all sorts of horrible things and be immoral. That's not what he meant. That's why the rest of the quote says, ". . . for the soul trained in love to God will do nothing to offend the One who is Beloved." St. Augustine believed that if you are so enraptured with God's love, if your heart is pointed in the direction of God's kingdom, if all you want is to know God and to love him, then, because of the transforming power of his love, you will naturally desire good. In other words, when you "do whatever you please," it will come out of a natural desire to always love your neighbor, do the right thing, and be a moral person, rather than having to look at a list of dos and don'ts.

In the Sermon on the Mount, Jesus says, "Do not think that I have come to abolish the Law or the Prophets; I have not come to abolish them but to fulfill them. For truly I tell you, until heaven and earth disappear, not the smallest letter, not the least stroke of a pen, will by any means disappear from the Law until everything is accomplished. Therefore anyone who sets aside one of the least of these commands and teaches others accordingly will be called least in the kingdom of heaven, but whoever practices and teaches these commands will be called great in the kingdom of heaven. For I tell you that *unless your righteousness surpasses that of the Pharisees and the teachers of the law, you will certainly not enter the kingdom of heaven*" (Matthew 5:17–20).

That last line is the most important in understanding Jesus' view of Scripture, about a righteousness that surpasses that of the Pharisees and the teachers of the law. In Jesus' day, Pharisees were considered the all-stars of religion. They were the ones who were considered to follow the Torah, God's law, better than anyone. Jesus says, you not only need to follow the Scripture to a T, but your righteousness needs to surpass those guys you think are living out the Torah.

Torah, which is the Jewish word for "law," is the center of Judaism. The Torah is beloved, is important, and is a wonderful thing. The Jews said the Torah, God's law, was like honey. In fact, it was "sweeter than honey" to the Jewish people in Jesus' day (Psalm 119:103). The synagogue back then, and still today, was centered on God's law, the Torah. They would take the scrolls containing God's words and dance and parade around the assembly, celebrating the greatness of the Scriptures. They would parade around with the Bible, and people would jump up and down celebrating, touching, reaching out to God's Scriptures because this was a sign of

God's covenant and love and instruction and way of life. It was the only way to live. Everyone in the synagogue would celebrate and desire and want the Torah, the law.

The entire educational system in Jesus' day was built around memorizing the Torah. Some of the students, when they became teenagers, memorized the complete *Tanakh*, which were the writings and the prophets. Psalm 1 says:

> Blessed is the one
>> who does not walk in step with the wicked
> or stand in the way that sinners take
>> or sit in the company of mockers,
> but whose delight is in the law of the LORD,
>> and who meditates on his law day and night.
> That person is like a tree planted by treams of water,
>> which yields its fruit in season
> and whose leaf does not wither—
>> whatever they do prospers. (vv. 1–3)

In this psalm we can see the Jewish view of the Torah—the law, God's Scripture, God's words—being such a central point to Judaism.

The Law of Sin and Death

For modern Christians who view themselves as free from the curse of the law (Galatians 3:13), Jesus' words about the Law and the Prophets— "not the smallest letter, not the least stroke of a pen"—can be confusing. Think of all of the writings of

Paul; for example, Paul says, "Therefore, there is now no condemnation for those who are in Christ Jesus, because through Christ Jesus the law of the Spirit who gives life has set you free from the law of sin and death" (Romans 8:1–2). What is "the law of sin and death"? Paul talks about it all the time: the law kills, the law destroys, the law is binding. This is confusing, isn't it? Here you have Jesus, at one point saying, "not the smallest letter, not the least stroke of a pen, will by any means disappear from the Law" and "anyone who sets aside one of the least of these commands . . . will be called least in the kingdom of heaven," and then you have Paul saying that it's the law of sin and death.

Also, look at Jesus. Jesus appears to break the Torah all the time, especially Sabbath law, doesn't he? You see him healing on the Sabbath, asking a blind man to wash his eyes on the Sabbath, denouncing the synagogue for spiritual blindness (John 9). You see his disciples eating kernels of grain on the Sabbath (Matthew 12:1–8). He is seemingly breaking all sorts of Torah law. This really needs some explanation if we're going to understand the Bible.

William Barclay's commentary says that the Torah, or law, can have four definitions.[1] The first definition is the first five books of the Bible: Genesis, Exodus, Leviticus, Numbers, and Deuteronomy. The second type of meaning of the law can mean something like the Ten Commandments or God's way. The third understanding of the law can mean the entire Old Testament. But the fourth understanding of the law, and the type that Paul is talking about when he calls it "the law of sin and death," is the oral tradition. You see, every Pharisee, rabbi, scribe, and teacher had a way in which they would interpret God's law as an application of life. These interpretations became oral tradition, forming factions and different traditions within the context of Judaism. These oral traditions would often vary depending on what religious group you were from. Each group had their own interpretation of what various passages meant for their readers. These interpretations were referred to as a rabbi's yoke.

It's like this: The Bible says we shouldn't work on the Sabbath and we should honor it. Nevertheless, the Bible doesn't necessarily say clearly how we're supposed to do that. So scribes, Pharisees, and teachers of the law would then come up with specific ways that you could "not work" on the Sabbath. For example, you shouldn't write two or more letters or extinguish a fire. These look like work, so they're forbidden. If you to go to Israel today, there are all sorts of rules like this. If you get on an elevator on the Sabbath, the elevator will stop on every floor so you don't have to push a button (since some would consider this work). The Bible doesn't say you can't press elevator buttons on the Sabbath, but one particular oral tradition does. They say, "Pressing elevator buttons on the Sabbath is work and therefore breaks God's law."

Does Scripture say anywhere in the Old Testament, "Thou shalt not press elevator buttons on the Sabbath"? No! It's just a part of oral tradition. These traditions were getting way out of hand in Jesus' day. Therefore, when Jesus talks about the Torah, he's talking about the Ten Commandments, God's way of life, and God's instruction. He's not talking about these other trappings, spiritual measurements of progress and discipline. God doesn't value a person by merit.

Now Paul—and this is important—is talking in large part to Gentiles who are coming to faith. Paul believes the Gentiles are under a new covenant, so they are omitted from signs of the old covenant because they've been grafted into that through Jesus. Signs of the old covenant—including circumcision, dietary laws, not weaving two types of cloth together, and so on—are not meant for Gentile Christians.

So going back, every rabbi and every scribe has an interpretation of the Torah, and they will explain that, for example, in order not to break the Sabbath, you don't spit. You have a rabbi and he's on the non-spitting campaign. That's what he's pushing for. He would say, "If you spit on Sabbath, you are breaking Scripture. If you spit on the Sabbath, you are not doing what the Bible says." How many of you hear similar things today from Christians? Christians do this all the time! All sorts of views in Christianity point at each other and say, "You're not being scriptural. You're breaking what the Bible says." How often do you see that? Like the Pharisees, these people believe that their interpretation of Scripture has become Scripture itself! When Jesus is talking about "not the smallest letter, not the least stroke of a pen," he's talking about the actual book, not about these particular interpretations and oral traditions.

Jesus then has his own interpretation of Scripture. That's what the "yoke" means. He says, "My yoke is easy and my burden is light" (Matthew 11:30). Jesus' interpretation of Scripture is the fullest, richest way to live. That's why he says that he has come to fulfill the law (Matthew 5:17). If you want to know what the Bible says, just be like Jesus. And to be like Jesus is for your righteousness to surpass that of the teachers of the law.

The Fullest, Richest Way to Live

How do we use the Bible in a way that is not legalistic, soul-killing, and judgmental? It's like this: When I started dating my at-the-time girlfriend, Hannah, I was like many men who are sometimes, shall we say, very dense. I loved Hannah dearly, but apparently, as we were dating, I wasn't doing whatever it is that boyfriends are supposed to do so that girlfriends feel loved.

So Hannah, who has five brothers, got an idea. She knew how clueless men are about romance. She put together a love list for me. I could tell she did a lot of work on this list. The list said, "What boyfriends do to show girlfriends they love them. Number one: They buy flowers or other romantic gifts from time to time. Number two: When the girlfriend has gone through a lot of work to look pretty, the boyfriend should compliment her. Number three: The boyfriend should open doors for the girlfriend at any possible time." That list was super helpful to me. I did everything on that list.

That well-used list eventually got crumply and old. Then there came a day when I realized there were many more ways to show my love that weren't on that list. I had come to a place in my relationship with Hannah that if I did only was on that list it wouldn't be enough. You might say that this list—how to love Hannah—was written on my heart. I don't have to refer to the list anymore. I certainly don't go around saying, "You know what? I ought to open doors for her." I don't say,

"Because I have this list, these are the only things I'm ever going to do for Hannah ever." Rather, the list was training wheels to make me a better boyfriend and, eventually, husband.

In many ways, Scripture is like this list. It's God coming to a particular people, the Jewish people, choosing to make a covenant with them, to make them his people. Then God gives them instructions on how to live. Still today, twelve years later, I think back on Hannah's list and it refocuses me. I think about it when Hannah and I are having trouble connecting or maybe the flame just isn't there. I think about all the things on that list, which I memorized. I know everything on it. I go back to the list to help me realign my relationship. The list is a tool, but the most important thing is Hannah! Likewise, the Bible is a tool, but the most important thing is Jesus! The Bible is not an end but a means to know him, to love him, to adore him, and to be like him. The dream then is to have all of Scripture written on your heart.

This is what St. Augustine meant when he said, "Love God and do whatever you please." If you love God and you know Jesus and you hang out with him and you spend time with him today, you won't want to offend him because you love him. You don't think about "not sinning." You think about loving God, and everything falls in its place.

A Changed Heart

Too often the goal of Christian living is about "not sinning" rather than about being totally passionate and zealous for God. It's like this: If I wanted to guide you to Moscow from LA I wouldn't say, "Don't go to London. Don't go to Rome.

Don't go to Paris. Don't go to New York. Now go. Oh, yeah, don't go to Bangladesh, either. No, no, don't go to Tokyo. Don't go to San Francisco." Right? If you go to Moscow, you're not going to go to Paris, you're not going to go to New York, and you're not going to go to London. If you connect with God and if you know God, then you will see quite clearly that you will have a changed heart. That's the huge difference between Jesus and the Pharisees.

One way to make this clear is to ask what a thief is. If you asked a Pharisee what a thief is, the Pharisee would likely say, "A thief is a person who stole something." If you asked Jesus what a thief is, he would say, "A thief is someone who would steal given the opportunity, even if he or she has never stolen. A thief is someone who has a thief's heart." That's what I believe. A Pharisee would say an adulterer is someone who commits adultery. Jesus would say an adulterer is someone who would cheat on his wife given the opportunity, whether or not he's done it. There is a huge difference between those two views.

Jesus is striving for more than just action, although he wants action. He wants to give his followers a new heart, a new will, a new way of viewing life, that given the opportunity, you wouldn't even want to do those things. That's what righteousness surpassing the Pharisees and teachers of the law means. There's no binding; there are no handcuffs; there's no wrestling. It's a newly created heart that, in the end, through training and knowing God and loving God and being close to him, you don't even want those things anymore. This new heart would say, "Of course I love my enemies. Of course I wouldn't lie. Of course I'm going to care for those who are in need. Of course I'm not going to worry." It's a natural part of the new creation that you are.

Jesus didn't come to bring a new law. He came to write the ideas and the fullness of his instruction on your heart, to make you a new creation. A Christian, then, is not necessarily someone who doesn't do this and does do that. A Christian is someone who is becoming just like Jesus. It's not about what you do and don't do. It's about becoming a person who is so enraptured in God's light and love that of course you're going to do the right thing. Your righteousness will far surpass that of the Pharisees and the teachers of the law. Not because you follow a set of rules; Pharisees do that. But you go way beyond rules into a flourishing joy, doing what you want—and what you want is good.

Words Written on Your Heart

In John 5:39–40 Jesus has this warning about striving to know the Scripture as an end in itself, without getting to know the God that Scripture points to. He says to the Pharisees, "You study the Scriptures diligently because you think that in them you have eternal life." But, he says, "These are the very Scriptures that testify about me, yet you refuse to come to me to have life."

I don't want to be the Christian who is diligently searching the Bible and yet cannot see, sense, or feel Jesus with his arm around my shoulder. I don't ever want to be that man.

You should love Scripture. You should memorize it. You should trust it. It is a rule of life. It is the words of God. It is infallible. It is powerful. It is righteous. It is worthy of study. The words of Scripture should be written on your heart. The Bible should draw you closer to Jesus, and it should make you a better person. Scripture should bring you to God's love and mercy and joy, and it should tell you and teach you a righteousness that surpasses that of the Pharisees and the teachers of the law.

The person Jesus is describing is the kind of person who says, "I love God so much that I would never do anything to offend him. Why would I do that? My life is so full and so rich and so flourishing. And I know that, even after I die, I will live. My life is eternal and pure and good. I didn't earn it; God gave it to me as a gift of grace, and I can't lose it."

You can become that kind of person. It all comes from loving God and receiving God's love over the years of your life, healing, renewing, restoring. My hope and belief is that you will become that person.

You have heard that it was said to the people long ago, "You shall not murder, and anyone who murders will be subject to judgment." But I tell you that anyone who is angry with a brother or sister will be subject to judgment. Again, anyone who says to a brother or sister, "Raca," is answerable to the court. And anyone who says, "You fool!" will be in danger of the fire of hell.

Therefore, if you are offering your gift at the altar and there remember that your brother or sister has something against you, leave your gift there in front of the altar. First go and be reconciled to them; then come and offer your gift.

Settle matters quickly with your adversary who is taking you to court. Do it while you are still together on the way, or your adversary may hand you over to the judge, and the judge may hand you over to the officer, and you may be thrown into prison. Truly I tell you, you will not get out until you have paid the last penny.

—Matthew 5:21–26

4 Anger Is Like a Headache

I WAS A PRETTY NICE GUY until the day I punched someone. It was in sixth grade. Until this fateful day I had always been amiable and friendly with those around me. I'm a big guy now, but I was a small guy then and was easily pushed around. I wasn't bullied often, but when I was I always acquiesced. A day came finally in sixth grade when, maybe by virtue of the onset of puberty, I'd had enough.

I was sitting at a picnic bench before school minding my own business. I was whistling while working on a homework assignment when a bully named Ryan said, "Hey, shut up. Stop whistling." For whatever reason I looked him square in the eyes, didn't say a thing, and continued whistling the theme song from *The Andy Griffith Show*, challenging him to do something about it.

Ryan was visibly angry. "I said, shut up!"

I kept whistling while looking at him square in the eyes.

With that, two of his comrades grabbed me by each arm and pulled me from my picnic bench. Ryan came over and started punching me in the stomach and chest when something came over me. I pushed the two kids away, and I landed a solid jab right under Ryan's nose. His head snapped back, feet flung into the air, and he dropped like a sack of potatoes. I stood over him victorious, both fists clinched. Then we did what all prepubescent boys do after a brief fight. We both started crying. Of course, by the end of the next week we were best friends.

I found a real power in my anger and violence. I felt like if I screamed loud enough or punched a guy in the face, I could get just about anyone to lay off. It felt good. Anger was also helpful as I was the "enforcer" on our hockey team at the local YMCA. When my anger went from repression to release, it was empowering and perhaps even healthy. But I allowed this anger to become rage and contempt. Before I knew it, I had become a little monster. By the early part of high school I had changed into a rotten person with a poisonous heart and was in desperate need of a saving Jesus.

The Issue of Anger

Anger is a normal, healthy part of life, but it is very dangerous and must be understood. The first moral issue Jesus tackles in the Sermon on the Mount is the issue of anger and its ability to turn its possessor into a person of contempt and even a child of hell.

He says, "You have heard that it was said to the people long ago, 'You shall not murder, and anyone who murders will be subject to judgment.' But I tell you that anyone who is angry with a brother or sister will be subject to judgment. Again, anyone who says to a brother or sister, 'Raca,' is answerable to the court. And anyone who says, 'You fool!' will be in danger of the fire of hell" (Matthew 5:21–22).

The first question Jesus raises is, who is a murderer? As we mentioned previously, the Pharisees would say, "A murderer is a person who has killed someone unjustly." Jesus, on the other hand, would say, "A murderer is someone who would murder if given the opportunity with no consequence." This cornerstone of the Sermon on the Mount cannot be over-emphasized. To Jesus, a murderer is someone who wants someone else dead. A murderer is not just a person who kills but someone who kills with words when they cannot do it with a sword.

The word *Raca* is a term of contempt. It is a rough, guttural word that sounds like someone is getting ready to spit. It is a way of lashing out at someone in anger, expressing they are "less than." In those days, saying "You fool" would be like cursing at someone. It would be like saying, "You stupid [insert expletive here]."

The moralists say, "Let's deal with murderers." But Jesus says, "No, let's deal with the murderous heart that comes from anger and rage. The best way to judge the heart is to judge the words that come from the heart." This is a very challenging teaching from Rabbi Jesus. At hearing this, I am forced to look at my heart and my words and ask if I am lining up with his call to have a "righteousness [that] surpasses that of the Pharisees and the teachers of the law" (Matthew 5:20). In fact, if I have a violent kind of a heart I am "in danger of the fire of hell" (v. 22).

Images of Hell

In the Bible there are four different words that are translated as "hell." The word Jesus uses here is *Gehenna*, the name of a valley just outside the city of Jerusalem where trash is burned. In Israel's history, this was a place where pagans did horrible things like sacrifice children to pagan gods. Because the Jews hated this place as a symbol of raw evil, they burned the city trash there. All the trash from the city would be carried out each day to this valley, not far from the city walls, and a fire would burn all day every day. It was a horrible place.

This is the image Jesus uses to talk about hell. There are two places: the City of God where God's righteous life-giving ways are experienced, and there is Gehenna, where things that don't belong in God's city go. Because the City of God is a place of peace and a place where God's love is experienced, those who have a heart of anger and contempt may be in danger of being thrust from the Holy City as a mercy to others. If you are mocking, laughing at, swearing at, or belittling others, you are working against God's redemptive work in the world. You are grouped with the violent ones who will be outside the City of God.

Understanding Anger

The soil from which all violence and contempt grows is anger. Understanding violence means understanding contempt, and understanding contempt means understanding anger.

Anger in itself is not evil. It isn't good or bad necessarily. Dallas Willard likens anger to a headache.[1] Its blessing is that it tells you something is wrong and needs to be addressed. It's like the blessing of pain: If my hand is numb and I place it on a frying pan, my hand will be destroyed. Because I have feeling, pain causes me to retract my hand instantly. Anger, like pain, should be an alarm that says, "Something is wrong!" You shouldn't praise anger as a virtue, nor should you feel ashamed when you feel it bubbling in your body. It is simply telling you to address something.

This alarm likely has less to do with the object of your anger than you think. If you find yourself, for example, angry at an inanimate object like a microwave, you can be guaranteed of this. There is something deeper going on with your anger than a piece of technology that doesn't work. If you find yourself angry several times a day, something deeper is going on in your soul and needs examining. Don't ignore it.

Anger happens when a personal limit is exceeded. This limit can be a boundary, it can be an unmet desire, it can be evil, or it can be something going on in your body like being hungry. In the end anger happens when we feel like someone has crossed our limits or our desires (sometimes we are that person—we cross ourselves). Anger then is a result of unmet desires. Anger is not a light switch we can simply turn off as we choose. Rather, when we want a desired outcome and it is derailed we cannot help but feel angry. Therefore, if we want to be less angry in our lives we have to address our limits, boundaries, and expectations. We cannot simply "try harder." In fact, in the long run, trying harder will probably only make things worse.

Addressing Anger

Because we can't address anger head-on, we must address it indirectly. For example, when I'm hungry I must eat something or I'm going to be impatient and rude.

Here are the top five biggest things that *indirectly* make us feel angry:

1. *Hurry.* If you are hurried, slow down. Hurrying comes from a place of pride and causes us to feel angry with those who are at peace in their lives.

2. *Stress.* If you are stressed about work, errands, or anything else, it's good to let go. We must fill our hearts and minds with what is really important in the kingdom of God. Most of the things we are stressed about are important but may not demand as much emotional energy as we are giving them.

3. *Worry.* If you are worried, be present. Entrust your future to God through prayer. Worrying will only make things worse. Relax in the shepherding of Jesus.

4. *Shame.* If you feel shame, then it's time to give yourself grace and forgiveness. You can't be a perfect parent or a perfect friend, and you cannot save the whole world. Keep appropriate boundaries and agree with God that you are his beloved. Sometimes we have to say no with love. Forgive yourself and release your shame.

5. *Entitlement.* We all are sick of everyone's entitlement, just not sick of our own. We all have desires, and desires are a good thing. Too often, however, our desires become expectations, and expectations become

entitlements. Expectation and entitlement poison our lives by removing surprise and joy. When our expectations are met, there is little joy because we got what we think was owed to us. This also means we are unlikely to express gratitude to those who gave or met a need. When we don't get what we think we deserve, we become livid. Therefore expectations and entitlements remove joy from our lives because they cause us to live with less gratitude and joy. What then are we to do?

Again, I look to Dallas Willard. His advice is for us to "abandon outcomes" to God. He echoes the cliché "Let go and let God."[2] If only we could actually do this. Abandoning outcomes is contrary to our pull-yourself-up-by-your-bootstraps culture. This culture is obsessed with particular outcomes for oneself or one's loved ones. Holding tightly to a particular good outcome is not the same as trusting God for his outcome. Abandoning outcomes is an act of faith that believes God can redeem any suffering, that anyone who trusts in God will ultimately be rescued and redeemed by him. It's time to let go of outcomes, which frees you to let go of your anger.

Release Your Anger

There is a certain power that comes with anger that can be almost pleasurable. If you've ever had that cathartic moment when you finally passionately say no, you know how good anger can feel. But feeling angry can become a part of our inner lives, a part of our body, where we feel angry and chew on it like a delicious meal. We don't just gulp it down like a dog eating bacon. No, we savor it, hang on to it as a treasure, and resist letting it go.

This is the real problem with anger: if we don't deal with anger, it can fester and eventually rot in our souls, turning us into contemptuous people whom others avoid.

This is why the apostle Paul says, "Do not let the sun go down while you are still angry, and do not give the devil a foothold" (Ephesians 4:26–27). Though the language is almost certainly metaphorical, I like to use this as a literal rule for my own spiritual development. In other words, I give myself a maximum of twenty-four hours before I need to find some kind of release for my anger. This means I have twenty-four hours to confront my adversary, to make amends, or to talk to a soul friend or even a therapist about how wounded I feel. This last piece is so important because you can have your anger validated and empathized. The way the soul and mind work is bizarre because sometimes this validation and empathy is all you need for your anger to evaporate.

When we are able to release our anger to a safe person we are given the freedom to do what we love and enjoy our life in God's kingdom, even though some things may still remain unresolved. Sometimes we can't resolve things with our adversaries because our emotional temperature is too high. So finding release for our anger actually brings us to a place of wholeness and sobriety of mind to help us work things out with those who make us angry.

A Plea for Reconciliation

Reconciliation is important to Jesus. In the Sermon on the Mount, he finishes his reflection on anger by pleading with his listeners to reconcile with the people we love. He gives this example: "If you are offering your gift at the altar and there remember that your brother or sister has something against you, leave your gift there in front of the altar. First go and be reconciled to them; then come and offer your gift" (Matthew 5:23–24). This is a powerful image. Offering your gift at the altar in the temple in Jerusalem was the highest religious experience a religious Jew could have. Jesus says that reconciling with your neighbor is a far greater way to show devotion to God than any other religious rite.

Nothing else pleases the heart of God more than to see his children, whom he loves, being reconciled to him and to each other. It pains the heart of God to see his kids angry at one another, gossiping and slandering one another, or committing violence by sword or by mouth. The entire life and ministry of Jesus is focused on reconciliation. If we want to be a part of his life, then we also must be a part of his ministry of renewal and reconciliation.

You have heard that it was said, "You shall not commit adultery." But I tell you that anyone who looks at a woman lustfully has already committed adultery with her in his heart. If your right eye causes you to stumble, gouge it out and throw it away. It is better for you to lose one part of your body than for your whole body to be thrown into hell. And if your right hand causes you to stumble, cut it off and throw it away. It is better for you to lose one part of your body than for your whole body to go into hell.

—Matthew 5:27–30

5 Missing the Mark

C HASTITY IS WONDERFUL. In an age of sexual freedom, when people see most moral boundaries around human sexuality as repressive and even unloving, there is a huge need for chastity. Until we understand chastity we cannot begin to understand a healthy sexuality.

When I say *chastity*, I don't mean *celibacy*. Celibacy means you don't have sex. Chastity means that your sexuality has boundaries so it can be more powerful. Yes, in order to have good sex you must also be chaste.

Chastity means human sexuality needs boundaries. And the reason it needs boundaries is not that sexuality is bad; it's not. It's an amazing thing. It needs boundaries to be more powerful. Søren Kierkegaard, a Danish philosopher and devout Christian, said, "Purity of heart is to will one thing."[1] Whether you're a man or a woman, no matter what your age, sexuality is an important part of your spirituality, and it requires boundaries and focus.

Lust and Adultery

The following passage is one of the most uncomfortable texts in the Sermon on the Mount. Jesus is talking about hell again. He's talking about looking at a woman lustfully as committing adultery, and more.

Jesus says, "You have heard that it was said, 'You shall not commit adultery.' But I tell you that anyone who looks at a woman lustfully has already committed adultery with her in his heart" (Matthew 5:27–28).

When Jesus says, "anyone who looks at a woman lustfully has already committed adultery with her in his heart," he doesn't mean sexually attracted. That would be every man on earth in human history. Men see beautiful women and look. They see the woman, they stare dumbly, they look away quickly as though they looked directly at the sun, and they forget her forever. Men by default are very much like golden retrievers looking at squirrels. They are going along and they see the squirrel, stare for a few seconds, then move on like it never happened. That kind of looking that men do, which is somewhat thick and brainless, is *not* what Jesus is talking about here.

So what does this mean: "Anyone who looks at a woman lustfully has already committed adultery with her in his heart"? First, don't think this is just for men. Any married person who looks lustfully at a person other than his or her spouse has committed adultery in his or her heart. This is because looking lustfully means to create within your heart a desire to sleep with that person or to create some kind of romantic bond. A man who has already committed adultery with a woman in his heart is a man who would sleep with that woman if given the opportunity. That's the point.

This is the big difference between legalism and the changed heart that we talked about in chapter 4. Legalism is the philosophy of the Pharisees, and the changed heart is the philosophy of Jesus. If you were to ask a Pharisee how he would describe an adulterer, a Pharisee would say, "An adulterer is one who has committed adultery." But if you were to ask Jesus how he would describe an adulterer, he would say, "An adulterer is someone who would commit adultery if given the opportunity."

Jesus' desire is to make moral and virtuous hearts. So an adulterer is someone who has fostered within him or herself a desire to be with someone else. Wives, if you're working with some guy in your office and you're becoming buddy-buddy with him and he is lavishing you with compliments and listening to you, and you're connecting, and now you're going out to lunch, and you think that if he made a move you might not mind so much—then you have the heart of an adulterer. Husbands, the same goes for you. If you are constantly fantasizing over a particular person, imagining what it would be like to be with her, and you know probably if you were given the opportunity you would sleep with her, then you have the heart of an adulterer.

Jesus wants to change our hearts so that we don't even want those things. And to be more specific, Jesus wants to change our hearts so that we want something even bigger and better, more thrilling, more exciting, and even more sexual.

Sacred Sexuality

Christian writers and philosophers have written about the idea of sexuality being something that's actually very spiritual. Ronald Rolheiser writes extensively on the issue in *The Holy Longing*.[2]

Believing in chastity means first believing that sexuality is much more than "having sex." Sexuality is a zeal, a passion, a fire within you that you are born with. It can be powerful and life-giving, or it can be destructive. The Greeks called this *eros*. Oftentimes Christians think eros is somehow corrupt because it's not the same as *agape*, the God kind of love. But eros is a good thing even though it is dangerous. It's a spiritual passion. Yes, eros leads to intercourse and sexuality, but it's so much more.

The word "sexual" comes from the Latin word *secarae*, which means "to cut out." An old church view of sexuality was that people longed to connect with one another after having been "cut out," not just in ways that meant having sex. This spiritual sexuality meant intimacy, relationships, meaningful friendships, connectivity, energy, and passion coming from an inner tearing—a desire to be connected with God and each other. In this view, sexuality is broader than genitalia or physical touching. Because we were born into a world that was cut out from God, we have a fire or a burning desire to connect with God and with each other. This desire is passionate, sometimes irrational, incredibly powerful, and cannot be ignored.

So this sexuality or eros, this spiritual power that everyone is born with, is an important part of who you are as a human being. Every person is born screaming, crying, and clawing. As we get older this power, this passion, this fire within us grows and as it grows, it becomes more dangerous. Therefore, this passion or this fire requires chastity. That is, it requires focus. It requires boundaries.

Suppose I asked you, "Is fire a good thing or a bad thing?" How would you respond? If Yosemite is on fire it's a bad thing. But if fire is used to make electricity it's a good thing. So, like fire, in order to have true power, your sexual passion requires focus because it's dangerous. Focus does not mean snuffing out the fire or even bringing its heat down. It means controlling it because it's hazardous. That passion in you is dangerous and needs to be respected, but not destroyed or diminished.

The Philosophy of Oneness

In its advent, Judaism brought oneness and health to a destructive pagan sexuality in the ancient Near East. When Judaism comes on the scene, "oneness" is the most important part of its message. The Jewish people came into a world of angry pagan gods, violent sexuality, drunkenness, and the occult. They brought something that was desperately needed: rules. The Jews brought a powerful idea. There are not hundreds of gods in the sky warring with one another, crazy, vengeful, and ready to destroy humanity at any moment. No, there is one God and his ways are right, good, and just. Jews, like Christians, would say there is one God. Christians would also say there is one baptism, there is one Eucharist, and there is one church.

The philosophy of oneness, and the boundaries that come with this philosophy, are not meant to destroy the power and the passion in life, but to give it power as if to take light and make it a laser. Christianity seeks to build chastity into the lives of Christ's disciples, to provide rules and boundaries around all the passions of life in general, thereby giving power for good and full living.

The Fullness of Focus

Our world is double-minded. We can't have everything because every decision is a thousand renunciations. Growing as a mature believer means understanding your limits and your inability to have everything. The tough reality is you can have one thing or nothing. And the more we break from this singularity, the more dangerous we are to ourselves and to others.

Many younger men today don't want to get married because they refuse to limit the amount of sexual variety. The constraint of only one partner is too much to handle. They despair at the thought of only one woman, even if she's incredibly beautiful. Unfortunately these men will never know the fullness of true sexuality if they don't experience married monogamy.

It's like this. Imagine putting corn seed in the ground. You bury it, it starts to grow a little, it comes out of the ground, and you think, *You know what, I don't want corn. I'm going to rip this out and throw it away. I want cabbage instead.*

So you put a cabbage seed in the ground and water it and take care of it. And then you think, *I don't want cabbage,* and throw it away.

I want to grow carrots.
Actually, I want tomatoes.
Actually, I want . . .

This is what people are doing today, not only with romantic relationships but also with any kind of commitment, whether it is a local church, a hobby, a degree, or a job. There's no devotion. There's no focus. There's no structure. But, in the example of romance, when a man chooses one woman, marries her, and makes her the focus of his life, he thinks, *I'm going to put an apple seed in the ground and I'm going to water it. I'm going to get apples and lots of them. I'm going to enjoy apple juice, apple jam, apple cider, and apple pie.*

And as he eats his apple pie he sees in the distance a lonely old man standing over piles of holes in the dirt, trying to decide whether he wants to grow carrots or corn.

In all aspects of life—and this is true of work, of art, of education—double-mindedness doesn't mean we get to have lots of things. It means we get to have nothing. Focus means we get to have one thing. Having lots of things is the lie because you never actually have them. It's only a fantasy.

Life's passion and zeal for existence require focus. We're so insatiable, we human beings. There's an inner brokenness, a fragmentation that just won't let us rest. We leave a long string of unfinished symphonies and festering regret. There are ways in which double-mindedness creates brokenness. Some of us are just never happy. So many of us never get to see the fullness of investing years of life into one thing. Rather we move from place to place, and person to person, never to see what devotion, chastity, and single-mindedness can do in life.

Desire Changes Your Vision

Dennis Prager tells a story about a man who said something was missing in his life. The missing thing in his life was hair on top of his head. He was bald. He said, "When I started going bald, all I could see were people with lots of hair everywhere."[3] His view of the world was completely altered by the fact he wanted to have hair. All he could see was a sea of people with hair, people who had what he wanted.

Desire changes your vision. When you're poor, it seems like everyone's rich. *Everyone else can do everything they want and I can't do anything.* There is something about human insatiability that makes us feel *I'm never rich enough, I'm never pretty enough, I'm never strong enough, I'm never young enough, I'm never liked enough.* That's not God's best.

Jesus says, "If your right eye causes you to stumble, gouge it out and throw it away. It is better for you to lose one part of your body than for your whole body to be thrown into hell. And if your right hand causes you to stumble, cut it off and throw it away. It is better for you to lose one part of your body than for your whole body to go into hell" (Matthew 5:29–30). I hope you know that Jesus doesn't mean he literally wants you to gouge your eye out or cut your hand off.

The Greek root for the word *stumble* is essentially "like a trap." It's a booby trap, as if you dug a hole in the ground, put branches on top of it, and then fell in.

Jesus says that if your eye or your hand keeps trapping you and destroying you, then just get rid of it. Better to throw the trap away than to throw your life away.

It's like a mosquito bite. You have this itch on your arm. You know this mosquito bite itches. Scratching it sounds so good, but if you scratch it, it's not going away. In fact it's going to itch more. Sometimes you just say, "Forget it!" and go nuts scratching. Then it gets inflamed and scabbed and itches even more.

This part of the human existence, this insatiability, this double-mindedness, is like a mosquito bite. Don't scratch it. Be single-minded, focusing on just one thing.

The Westminster Shorter Catechism says, "The chief aim of man is to glorify God and enjoy him forever." Now the reason that's so important is because when your life is about glorifying God, everything that is good and life-giving comes out of you. And everything that is life thwarting and destructive goes away. The purpose of my marriage is to glorify God. The purpose of my work is to glorify God. The purpose of my hobbies, gatherings, art, and reflection is to glorify him. Everything I do is to glorify God in this world and to enjoy him forever!

That's what all of this is about. The purpose of human existence is to know God and to glorify him. This doesn't make sense to those who don't really know God. It may seem esoteric, but to know God, to glorify him, and to enjoy him forever is the one thing we were all born to do. That is where eternal life comes from.

• •

It has been said, "Anyone who divorces his wife must give her a certificate of divorce." But I tell you that anyone who divorces his wife, except for sexual immorality, makes her the victim of adultery, and anyone who marries a divorced woman commits adultery.

—Matthew 5:31–32

• •

6 Healing Broken Families

I N OUR STUDY of the Sermon on the Mount, we arrive at one of the most difficult passages to read from Jesus' sermon. As I prepared to write this chapter, I suffered as I thought about the thousands of people who would read these words about divorce. There are so many scenarios where couples split, every story painful and unique. How could I paint a broad stroke?

This is a deeply personal chapter as well, because my parents divorced when I was three years old. All of us have been touched by the wounds of broken relationships. Whether you've been through a separation or you've been affected by broken marriages of others, be it your parents, your kids, or a good friend, we all know there's something really sad and difficult about its tearing nature. If you've split with a spouse, I don't want you to read this and feel guilty. That would only make things worse for your soul. If you have parents or kids who have been through a divorce, don't feel self-righteous toward them. All of us who have been touched in some way by divorce can feel restored, can receive a touch from the great healer Jesus Christ, who can redeem and bring health and healing to any story.

God's Intent for Marriage

Before we talk about divorce we need to talk about marriage. Marriage begins in Genesis 2. God creates the universe out of the void. In it he puts this planet and on that planet he puts Adam. Adam is made from the dust of the Garden of Eden and receives the breath of God. God instructs Adam to take care of this garden and to care for everything in it. Adam then becomes a visibly lonely man. He needed a partner, a woman.

God sees Adam and says that it's not good for him to be alone. Then God brings animals before Adam. We think this was Adam's first job, naming the animals. However, at a close reading of the text, we actually see that God is presenting these animals before Adam to be his helper or his mate:

"The LORD God said . . . 'I will make a helper suitable for him.' Now the LORD God had formed out of the ground all the wild animals and all the birds in the sky. He brought them to the man to see what he would name them; and whatever the man called each living creature, that was its name. So the man gave names to all the livestock, the birds in the sky and all the wild animals. But for Adam no suitable helper was found" (Genesis 2:18–20).

So by naming them, Adam is essentially rejecting each one of the animals as his helper. He is essentially saying, "This is not Eve, this is 'Cat.' This is not Eve, this is 'Alligator.'"

One after another, each animal comes before Adam, he rejects these animals, and finally he says that none of them was a suitable helper. God then puts Adam to sleep and takes a rib from him. We know the story. God creates woman. You then get this sense that, as Adam wakes up, he sees a woman, a naked woman at that, in the garden, and he says, "This is now bone of my bones and flesh of my flesh" (Genesis 2:23). He's found his helper. He's found the one he's been looking for.

When Adam and Eve come together, there is a union as these two are invited to be a part of God's creative work on earth, even before the Fall. Think about procreation. Adam and Eve, by God's power, can now create other human souls! When they come together, they can create a human being who comes into this world as an eternal being. So procreation is an essential part of God's work. There's also the idea of stewardship. Adam and Eve are going to co-steward this person, raise up children, and take care of one another. Intimacy is the idea of loving one another, caring for one another, and being there for one another. This is all a part of marriage. This is all a part of what God intends for Adam and Eve.

So the idea of the incarnational reality of God's love, essentially, is that Adam can most feel God's love through Eve. Adam says, "I can do for someone else what God does for me. I can do this for Eve by caring for her, creating with her, and stewarding life with her." Eve says the same thing: "I am brought into God's creative, redemptive process with

Adam because I can care for him and love him." So God's love now is most tangibly felt in marriage, ideally. That's the idea behind two coming together. It's the idea that the fullness of God's love, God's creative nature, God's intimacy, and God's power would be experienced in marriage.

The Reality of Divorce

We must understand God's intention for marriage before we measure divorce. Nobody wanted divorce when they envisioned marriage to the man or woman of their dreams. Everybody wants a thriving, full, happy marriage where you rent movies and get ice cream together and go to Disneyland and have happy kids, and live life together until you just die together in old age. However, too often marriage is nothing like what we thought it would be. And that's one of the hardest things about divorce. You are essentially acknowledging that all your hopes and dreams from that happy day years ago when you were first married have been crushed. You're dying to those old dreams. They're not going to come about in the way you thought they would. And not only do you have to deal with that, but also everybody else has to deal with that.

Jesus says, "It has been said, 'Anyone who divorces his wife must give her a certificate of divorce.' But I tell you that anyone who divorces his wife, except for sexual immorality, makes her the victim of adultery, and anyone who marries a divorced woman commits adultery" (Matthew 5:31–32).

God implemented this idea of the certificate of divorce in Levitical law. And the principle of the Levitical law was simply this: God wanted people to have thriving, full, happy, ice-cream-eating marriages. However, in Moses' day and Jesus' day, women were not treated as most women are today in the modern West. Women were just short of being property of the husband or father. In Moses' day, in particular, if the man had no way to divorce a wife, then he could beat his wife black and blue.

The certificate of divorce was a way that a violent man could release his wife, saving the woman from the harm of the wicked man. She could then use this certificate to salvage some part her reputation. It was a very practical way of protecting women. Yet from that came a new sort of legalism in which a man could divorce a woman for any reason.

There were, at the time, two Jewish sects that argued for this legalism. The first view is called Shumai. A Shumai rabbi said you could divorce your spouse if he or she commits adultery. That makes sense.

However, another group called Hallel said, "Men, you can divorce your wife for any reason you want." They even went as far as to say that if you see a woman who's prettier than your wife, you can divorce her. If she puts too much salt on your food, you can divorce her.

In Jesus' day, if a woman was divorced she was ruined. She was viewed as property, remember. A divorced woman had one of three options. The first and best option was to remarry (very unlikely unless she was a total knockout). However, even in this scenario, she was viewed as used goods, and her new husband could hang it over her head and quite likely would. The second option: she could become a prostitute or a beggar, and that often would happen. Imagine this scenario: you're a married woman, you have your kids, you have a life, and one day your husband says your food is too salty and throws you out on the street. You have nowhere else to go but living on the streets. Number three: believe it or not, the worst option was to go back to your own family. In those days if you went back to your own family, you were considered a disgrace and essentially became like a slave in the household. I don't know why that's worse than prostitution, but apparently it was.

So there is a justice element in Rabbi Jesus' teaching. Jesus is angry at the rampant divorce of his day, watching women being thrown out to the vultures.

Divorce Is Not God's Ideal

There is still another part of divorce that really hurts and wounds God. It's simply this: divorce wasn't God's vision when he brought together you and your spouse, or your parents, or your kid and your kid-in-law. Everyone believed this marriage would become a thriving family with happy children and everything would be great. This was what God wanted too: a happy marriage and a full life. Then something happens and it doesn't work out.

Jesus says something important in Matthew 19:

> Some Pharisees came to him to test him. They asked, "Is it lawful for a man to divorce his wife for any and every reason?"
>
> "Haven't you read," he replied, "that at the beginning the Creator 'made them male and female' and said, 'For this reason a man will

leave his father and mother and be united to his wife, and the two will become one flesh'? So they are no longer two, but one flesh. Therefore what God has joined together, let no one separate."

"Why then," they asked, "did Moses command that a man give his wife a certificate of divorce and send her away?"

Jesus replied, "Moses permitted you to divorce your wives because your hearts were hard. But it was not this way from the beginning. I tell you that anyone who divorces his wife, except for sexual immorality, and marries another woman commits adultery." (vv. 3–9)

From the beginning divorce was not God's ideal for people who are married.

When two people become one flesh, they cannot be neatly and cleanly separated. All of us who have been in the midst of divorce know this. The marriage covenant doesn't separate; it tears, it breaks, and it bleeds. If you've been through a divorce, you know how ugly and dirty it can be. Everything splits, not only you and your husband or you and your wife, but also your kids. Your kids now are going back and forth. Then they may get new stepdads and stepmoms. Your friends get split and they have to pick. And your families used to be close, but now things are awkward. You have to split baptisms and split weddings and split everything. Everything is split, everything is broken, everything is wounded. And it's not just you and your spouse, but your whole community is split. Everything breaks and tears and it's never clean and it never feels good. All of us then have been wounded in some way by divorce and broken families.

I was three years old when my parents split. I don't even remember my parents being married. My earliest memory is holding my grandma's hand, looking for an Easter egg. I think during that time, my parents were still married. But I really don't remember them being married. They were eighteen and nineteen when they got married. They were young, but they stuck it out and did their best. They were married for nearly ten years. When they got divorced, my dad was a pastor and his church had to deal with the fact that they now had a divorced pastor in a time when divorce was even more frowned upon than it is now. Also my mom had to leave the church community that had been such a central part of her life. It was a mess.

On top of that, there is this wound that I've carried, even as an adult. It's the complication of having two families and choosing between them. My whole life I've had to choose. For example, on Christmas, I have to choose. On Easter, on Thanksgiving, on the Fourth of July I have to choose. My whole life has been this feeling. I know I shouldn't let it bother me, but it does. I wonder if each side of the family thinks I love the other side more.

When my dad married Donna, who is incredible, and when my mom married Ron, who is also incredible, they started having kids together and so they made these new families. No matter how loving they are to me, no matter how hard they try to reach out to me, there is a spot in my heart that never feels 100 percent a part of either family. I always feel like I'm 50 percent a part of each family. And it's not their fault! It's just all me! Here I am in my thirties with kids of my own, and I'm still thinking diplomatically about where I'm going to go on Christmas. Every time I see a family photo I'm not in, it still hurts somehow. And there's nothing I can do about it. I'll take it with me to my grave.

God's Offer of Grace

The thing about divorce and about all of our relationships is that they're not trivial. They touch those who are around us. God doesn't want divorce.

Now some people should absolutely get a divorce. I can say with spiritual authority as a pastor that if there is destructive sexual behavior, if there is abuse, which I think is what Jesus means by "hardness of heart" in Matthew 19, if there is abandonment, then you have every right to get a divorce. But it's still going to hurt.

If you're married to someone who is abusive, you should divorce him or her. Maybe you already did, and you haven't forgiven yourself, so you still feel guilty. Maybe your former spouse hangs it over your head. Maybe your parents got a divorce and you're still holding it against them. Maybe you're currently going through a divorce and you don't want to do it, yet it's still happening to you. Maybe your kids or grand-kids are going through a divorce and you feel disappointed with them.

In John 4, Jesus is sitting at a fountain with a Samaritan woman and he says, "Go, call your husband and come back" (v. 16). And she says, "I have no husband" (v. 17). He says, "You are right when you say you have no husband. The fact is, you have had five husbands, and the man you now have is not your husband" (vv. 17–18). And this is the part that I want you to understand. He knows her relationship history, and he offers her rivers of living water. This woman has been divorced not just once, but five times. He offers her rivers of living water.

All of us have been wounded. And if you haven't, you're lying to yourself. It's just what happens in life—from being bullied in school, to not getting the girl or the guy you thought you would get, or divorce, or death. We think, *I will never be whole again. My relationships will never work out ever again.* Yet God offers us rivers of living water, of new life.

Here's the thing: the past is the past. Grace is offered no matter how many horrible mistakes you've made, whether it is in getting married or getting divorced, or whatever it is you've done, grace is offered to all of us who have messed up. Grace is offered to your parents. Grace is offered to your children. Grace is offered to your ex-wife and your ex-husband. Grace is offered to you—and with it, rivers of living water.

If you are remarried, commit yourself to your new relationship, to your new spouse. If you think you will never have a relationship again, commit yourself to becoming the type of person who can take in God's love and show it to another person. You can be redeemed in your relationships, you can be redeemed in your brokenness, and you can be redeemed in your woundedness. And you can also be a source of grace to others.

That's another piece. You may have no idea how meaningful it would be to your parents who have been divorced, or your children who've been divorced, or your sibling who's been divorced, to just give them grace and love and forgiveness and encouragement. They don't need guilt. They have plenty of that, trust me.

That's what God offers us every day. He offers all of us, in the midst of our brokenness, rivers of living water. Allow God to heal your wounds.

Again, you have heard that it was said to the people long ago, "Do not break your oath, but fulfill to the Lord the vows you have made." But I tell you, do not swear an oath at all: either by heaven, for it is God's throne; or by the earth, for it is his footstool; or by Jerusalem, for it is the city of the Great King. And do not swear by your head, for you cannot make even one hair white or black. All you need to say is simply "Yes" or "No"; anything beyond this comes from the evil one.

—Matthew 5:33–37

7 The Easy, Honest Life

I WAS TELLING SOME FRIENDS about a time I had lunch with Val Kilmer . . .

"So Val and I were having lunch, you know, bagel sandwiches and whatnot. Val was telling me about his new Moses play and I was weighing in on his view of Moses. After a while we started talking about Mary Baker Eddy and comparing his view on Christian Science with my own Christian views. It was fun for both of us. We were laughing a lot. He's a great guy."

Later, my cousin said, "What was that about?"

"What?" I replied dumbly.

"I was there when you 'met' Val Kilmer."

All of sudden I felt my blood go cold. I forgot my cousin was there when I met Val Kilmer. It wasn't a lunch either. It was a brief meeting of about three minutes where I asked him to sign my copy of *Tombstone*. No, I didn't even ask him. I just held the DVD out to him stupidly and didn't even say anything. He signed it, greeted us kindly, and walked away. My cousin knew this and I was caught. Being caught lying is the worst feeling in the world.

The Danger of Dishonesty

Let's talk about lying—not only the way we lie to others, but the way we lie to ourselves. We so easily fall into the trap of deceiving, faking, posturing, and pretending.

If you bought something recently, it had a price tag, which is a relatively new invention. The Quakers, who came about in the nineteenth century, didn't like bargaining. It's an interesting thing. Up until 1860 or so, if you wanted to buy something, you'd go to a store. You'd have some money, and then you'd negotiate back and forth.

You'd say, "I want to buy your horse."

The seller would say, "Okay, well, this is a nice horse. I'll sell it to you for five hundred dollars."

"Five hundred dollars? I've only got fifty."

"Okay, four fifty."

"Well, you know, I've only got one hundred dollars in my pocket so that's as high as I can go."

Like a game, negotiating was a way of lying to one another, back and forth.

The Quakers believed that this type of dishonest haggling was distasteful and that it bothered the heart of God. So the price tag was invented because Quakers didn't want to quibble over costs. That idea came from the Sermon on the Mount. The Quakers, even today, won't take an oath in court. Their concept is that they want everything about their speech, how they talk, how they trade, everything they do to be 100 percent honest and forthright. They saw it, and still see it, as a cornerstone of Christian living.

In the Sermon on the Mount Jesus says to those listening, "You have heard that it was said to the people long ago, 'Do not break your oath, but fulfill to the Lord the vows you have made.' But I tell you, do not swear an oath at all: either by heaven, for it is God's throne; or by the earth, for it is his footstool; or by Jerusalem, for it is the city of the Great King. And do not swear by your head, for you cannot make even one hair white or black. All you need to say is simply 'Yes' or 'No'; anything beyond this comes from the evil one" (Matthew 5:33–37).

When he says, "You have heard that it was said to the people long ago . . ." he's referring to Levitical law. This was not just a law about how you lived your life, but how the Jewish state was going to govern itself—in court and every other way. So the oath, like our oaths in court, was to keep people honest in their judicial testimonies.

In court today witnesses take an oath to God with our hand on the Bible. We know that if we break that oath, we've perjured ourselves in court. It was true then and we still have that rule today.

So when this law was made, you could essentially prosecute people if they misspoke or lied within a court of law. It then wove its way into the moral fabric of how the Jewish people lived their daily lives. Those looking for it were able to find a loophole. Somebody looking at the law could say, "Well, if the law says if I make an oath to the Lord and I break it, then I'm in trouble. But I presume that also means that if I don't make a promise in the name of the Lord, then I'm fine." With this moral gray area people would lie and deceive because they could shrug their shoulders and say, "Well, I didn't swear anything to the Lord. I didn't make any promise."

If a person was known to be dishonest and there was some kind of transaction going on, he or she would simply say something like, "I swear by Jerusalem." That sounds like the person is swearing by God, right? The other person would think, *Okay, if he swears by Jerusalem, he's bound.* Then later the buyer says, "You lie! You swore by Jerusalem." But the seller responds, "Aha! I swore by Jerusalem, not by the Lord!" You see the tricky nature of this oath? People would say, "I swear by heaven," "I swear by the earth," "I swear by my head."

The original idea of swearing to the Lord in Levitical law was to remember that God is a part of the transaction. So when Jesus says in this text that heaven is God's throne, the earth is his footstool, Jerusalem is his city, and the hair on your head is his, he means that every word you say, every transaction you make, everything you do, God is a part of it. God isn't only a part of your conversation when you invoke him. Jesus is reminding his listeners that no matter what they do in life, God is a part of their living.

So what he's asking for is a different kind of person, a person who wants pure honesty all the time. A person whose reputation and character are so strong that no one would dare ask for an oath because they know he or she is an honest person. Jesus is trying to get rid of this "letter of the law" stuff that creates loopholes and instead wants to create people who are just plain honest. Imagine that.

Why Do We Lie?

Deception is woven into our culture. Most of us lie first and then think about it after we do it. We lie and think, *Oh, maybe I shouldn't have done that.* It's a natural thing we do usually to get out of trouble or to get people to like us.

A study conducted by Robert Feldman at the University of Massachusetts found that in an average ten-minute conversation, a typical person would lie three times.[1] The funniest part of the study is that they knew when people were lying in the survey. The first question they asked was, "Are you a liar?" Ninety-seven percent of the people who were taking the survey said, "No, I am not a liar." And 3 percent of the people who were taking this test said, "Yeah, I'm a liar." After the review, the 3 percent who admitted to being liars were 30 percent more honest throughout the whole exam than the 97 percent who said they weren't liars.

Most of the time when you lie, it's just a little white lie and you probably don't really think about it. You talk about how fast you were, where you were at work, or what this person said or how much you sold your house for, how well your kids are doing.

Every one of us lies. Why do we do this? Why do we feel so trapped into leading dishonest lives and lying about ourselves, and our families, and our friends, and what we do? There are two contradictory needs.

Our Need to Be Good

First of all, every single human being has an inner need to be good. You have a part of your nature that needs to be a good person.

If I sat someone down and said, "Joe, you are not a happy person," or "You are not a nice person," or "You're not a funny person," Joe might say, "Okay, fine." But if I said, "Joe, you are not a good person," that strikes much deeper than anything else, right? Joe would respond with either, "Yes, I am a good person," or, "You just don't understand me." What person would say, "I agree with you. I am not a good person"? Every bad guy thinks he's the good guy. Any person who is evil thinks he or she is at least average on the goodness scale. If you ask them about the evil things they do, they would go through all sorts of mental gymnastics and justifications because people tend to think they are good.

Our Need to Be Loved

That need to be good is in conflict with another need—the need to be loved. Both of these needs are from God. But that need to be loved can look like a need to be accepted, a need to be popular, a need to be in the inner circle, a need to be home. We need to be loved. And there is a narrative in which our need to be loved is at odds with our need to be good! What do I mean by that?

Let me explain. The vast majority of people who love me, Bobby Schuller, have a point at which they're going to stop loving me based on what I do or don't do. So do you. You may think I'm a funny guy. Well, what happens if I stop being funny? Will you love me then?

Sure, I'll love you.

Well, you may think I'm a nice guy. What happens if I'm not as nice? Will you still love me?

Yeah, we'll still love you.

What happens if my manners go and now I'm a rude person? Do you still love me?

Uh-huh, yeah.

Now, what if I steal from you? You don't love me anymore, do you?

Well . . .

What if I'm violent? What if I gossip about you? What if I hold contempt in my heart for you?

All of us have a deep fear of not being in that circle or in that group of friends or part of that clique. This is a deep need that often finds itself at odds with our need to be good. Well, what do we do? Typically we figure out that our reputations need a little management. To say the least, many of us are obsessed with the need to manage our reputations. If you are a professor at a college, you have to publish or perish, and you have to let people know about your connections. If you're a pastor of a church, you have to keep your church full. You have to keep the money coming in. You have to preach good sermons.

There are all sorts of ways in which we posture, buy things, and do things to manage our reputations out of our need to be loved. Each time, we sacrifice just a little bit of our need to be good.

Managing Our Reputations

When I was a kid, I went to Ambuehl Elementary School in San Juan Capistrano, where they had these things called the golden eagles. If you did something good, you were given a golden eagle. And if you got ten golden eagles, you became a golden eagle student. I remember the first time I got a golden eagle I showed my dad and he congratulated me on being so good. So I started really trying to get more golden eagles. I was so excited about this because I got attention from my dad, and rightly so. Every time I got a golden eagle, I showed it to him and he was so supportive.

One day when I was in second grade, I was throwing rocks against a wall and a teacher came over and gave me a demerit, which removes three golden eagles. Not only that, but I had to get my demerit signed by a parent and then bring it back to the teacher. And, oh, my day was horrible. I thought about the great reputation I had with my dad. I'd had seven golden eagles, but now I was back down to four. All my progress was gone. And not only that, I had to tell him that I got a demerit for throwing rocks against a wall. And I remember wondering how I could get around this.

Because my parents were divorced I had a card to play. I knew my mom wouldn't really care, so I held on to the demerit and I got Mom to sign it instead of Dad. My goal was to get thirteen golden eagles and then say I just received ten. That was my strategy.

Nevertheless, my dad found the demerit—and you should have seen me. I was like a deer caught in headlights. My mind raced. *How do I fix this?* Then I started crying. Dad said, "It's okay. You threw some rocks at a wall. I don't care. It's fine." He was really loving and gracious.

Many of us live with the constant need to manage our reputation and image. In order to be loved and perceived as good, we lie about or exaggerate our merits, while hiding our flaws, intentionally deceiving others so they won't see our warts. We carefully lie and manage our reputation because of our need to be included. Yet here's the great irony: the worst thing for your reputation is to be caught in a lie.

As you go further down that hole with a pattern of lying, you create a spiritual and psychological burden that gets heavier and heavier. It becomes a weight you don't even realize you're carrying. You have this big thing on your back and you wonder what's going on. Yet you've forgotten completely because you've been carrying it for so long. You're living a life of people pleasing, managing your reputation, and lying.

The very worst is when you lie to yourself. That's when things get really bad, and we've all done it. This is described best in Dostoyevsky's *The Brothers Karamazov*. At the beginning of the story, the main character Alyosha, a monk, has this boorish father. They call him a buffoon. Now the father somehow gets an audience with an elder, who is Alyosha's mentor, and sort of begins mocking the elder. The elder chastises the father, who asks for forgiveness and repents profusely (at this point the reader doesn't know if the father is being genuine).

The elder says, "Above all, do not lie to yourself. A man who lies to himself and listens to his own lie, comes to a point where he does not discern any truth either in himself or anywhere around him, and thus falls into disrespect towards himself and others. Not respecting anyone, he ceases to love. And having no love, he gives himself up to passions and course pleasures in order to occupy and amuse himself. And in vices, he reaches complete bestiality and it all comes from lying to others and to himself."[2]

We don't have to live this way. We don't have to build a fake image or a shiny reputation. We don't have to lie. Many are so far down that path, when they think about being honest people, being who they truly are, being open about what's going on in their soul, they are horrified to think about the world actually seeing their naked true selves. If this is you, a part of you says, "Oh, it would be so freeing to just be myself," but the fear is also so gripping. *What would it be like to let people actually see this part of me?*

The Messy Process of Becoming Honest

Recently we started spring-cleaning the house. It's a horrible process. The house seems clean, but when you want to deep clean the house, it gets filthy! That's precisely what happens. You go through the drawers, and you go under the bed, and you go behind the fridge. Your house looked clean before you started cleaning, but now that you're spring-cleaning, all of a sudden it's as if the Tasmanian devil just came through and ruined everything. That's what you have to do in order to truly clean your house. It always gets messier before it gets cleaner.

If you have a lot of stuff hidden in your life and stored away, it's going to be a messy ordeal ahead of you. But the alternative is to be like a house that's never clean, a burden that's never dropped, and a heart that is never at peace. Is that what you want?

One of the best moments is when you actually come out about these struggles, these wounds, and the things you've been lying about. When you stop managing your reputation, you realize that people actually sometimes love you more when you're honest. Not only is your wound connected to their wound, which is a wonderful thing, but they trust you more and they see the real you.

If you have been pretending, people already know you're not being honest. So when you begin to live honestly and speak honestly, which requires training and practice and grace and love, people will respond to you in ways that will be really healing to your soul. I promise you that.

The most important thing to remember is this: something has to change inside us, about the way we view ourselves and the way we view love, in order for us to stop leading this dishonest, reputation-managing existence.

The Freedom of an Honest Life

There's something about God's love. He knows everything about you. He's with you now. Your whole life he's going to be walking alongside you. He sees all the stuff you do. He sees all the wounds you might even be blind to. And part of changing is learning to live in that love of God that says, "You're not what you do, you're not what you have, and you're not what people say about you. You're my child. There's nothing that can take that away from you. I love you, dear child."

You see, the more you dwell in that kind of love, you start to realize and recognize what real love is. This love is abiding and full of grace . . . when you're honest.

So this is what Jesus is saying to us in the Sermon on the Mount. He wants a changed heart, a heart that says, "I am sick of lying, I am sick of managing my reputation, I am sick of deceiving people, of twisting the truth to manipulate people, to get what I want. I'm giving that up. I'm abandoning that. I don't care if people think I'm holy. I don't care if people think I'm rich or beautiful, or smart, or cool, or funny. I don't care if I'm likable. From this day forward, I decide to live in the easy yoke of Jesus, in which I can just be an honest person all the time."

And you can. If you do that, so much worry and stress and anxiety and fear will just melt away from your life. A heavy burden will lift from your back like a bunch of balloons going into the sky. Trust me. God loves you and that's the only thing that matters.

You have heard that it was said, "Eye for eye, and tooth for tooth." But I tell you, do not resist an evil person. If anyone slaps you on the right cheek, turn to them the other cheek also. And if anyone wants to sue you and take your shirt, hand over your coat as well. If anyone forces you to go one mile, go with them two miles. Give to the one who asks you, and do not turn away from the one who wants to borrow from you.

—Matthew 5:38–42

8 Courageous Peacemakers

EUGENE PETERSON, AUTHOR OF *The Message* para-phrase of the Bible, tells a story about when he was a kid growing up as a Christian. His mom taught him, "Eugene, when you're at school, if anybody ever picks on you, you need to turn the other cheek." For him, that meant avoiding the bullies but still getting beat up all the time. One bully picked on Eugene endlessly, and every time Eugene thought, *I've got to turn the other cheek. I've got to be a Christian. I've got to be a good guy.*

One day, he lost it and decided to go beat up this kid. Eugene fought back and realized he was much stronger than the bully, which came as a big surprise. He took the bully to the ground, straddling his chest and hitting him on the face. Eugene said to the kid, "Say uncle, say uncle!"

The bully said, "No, I won't say uncle!"

Eugene hit him again. "Say uncle!"

The bully said, "No, I won't say uncle."

Then Eugene remembered his faith, so he said, "Say Jesus Christ is my personal Lord and Savior!"

The bully cried out, "Jesus Christ is my personal Lord and Savior!"

Eugene Peterson said, "That was my first convert to Christianity."[1] It's a great story.

What happens with bullies? What happens with evil? What happens with injustice? One of the things that is misunderstood about the Sermon on the Mount is that, in the case of Eugene Peterson, Jesus' teaching is neither for Eugene Peterson to cower and to hide, nor is it for him to fight the bully by straddling him on his chest and punching him in the face. In this passage, Jesus is suggesting a third alternative that requires more courage, more dignity, and more nobility than fight or flight. To live this way in the kingdom of God doesn't mean to be a coward, and it doesn't necessarily mean to fight. It means that there is a better, nonviolent alternative to resolve conflict.

A New Approach to Enemies

God loves your enemies. Now that may surprise you. He loves you, as well, and that's the good news. But because God's love for us is so great, he wants to use us as a reconciliatory agent to our enemies and that requires great courage, great nobility, and great strength of character. It means that your honor has to come from God and not from man. That's where this all begins.

Remember at the beginning of his sermon, Jesus looks at a bunch of hurting, broken people, and he says, "I want you to be salt and light. I want you to live in a different reality where your honor, your wealth, and your strength—the fullness of your life—come from knowing the Father. I want to empower you to be a different kind of person in this world."

Jesus says, "You have heard that it was said, 'Eye for eye, and tooth for tooth.' But I tell you, do not resist an evil person. If anyone slaps you on the right cheek, turn to them the other cheek also. And if anyone wants to sue you and take your shirt, hand over your coat as well. If anyone forces you to go one mile, go with them two miles. Give to the one who asks you, and do not turn away from the one who wants to borrow from you" (Matthew 5:38–42).

Now, this passage has very little to do with dealing with enemies through the police or the military. This has everything to do with the way you interact with your personal enemy in your own life.

Turn Your Cheek

Notice Jesus says, "If someone slaps you on the right cheek." Not just the cheek, but the right cheek. Why did he specify the right cheek? That seems weird to us. But everybody in Jesus' audience knew exactly what kind of a slap a right-cheek slap is. It's not a violent slap—it is an insulting slap.

Let me explain. In Jesus' day, people didn't use the left hand. Jewish custom says don't use the left hand to eat, don't use it to shake hands with someone, and don't even use it to slap somebody. They used the right hand. So in Judaism, the right hand is the hand of power and the left hand is the hand of weakness.

97

In Genesis 48, we read the story of Jacob blessing his grandsons Ephraim and Manasseh, and his son, Joseph. Manasseh is on Jacob's right side and Ephraim is on his left side, because Joseph wants his father to bless them in that order. But Jacob crosses his hands to put his right hand on Ephraim and his left hand on Manasseh. Joseph tries to explain that Manasseh is the firstborn. Jacob says, "I know. . . . Nevertheless his younger brother [the one on his right hand] will be greater than he" (v. 19). So you see the hand is really important. If you were going to slap someone, or eat, or point at something, or write, you would use your right hand.

There is only one way to slap someone on the right cheek with the right hand. You have to backhand slap them.

A backhanded slap in Jesus' day was not a regular slap or hit or violent attack. It was an insult. It would be like spanking somebody. It was what you did to children and slaves; it's what you did to people who were beneath you.

So imagine now a peer of yours comes up to you and backhands you in the face. By this gesture he is saying, "You are less than me. You are like a slave or a child or a piece of property. You are less than human to me. I backhand you." Remember in Jesus' day, this is a society based on shame and honor. To receive honor from someone was a great thing, and to receive shame from someone was a horrible thing. It was a terrible thing for a peer of yours to come up to you and backhand you in the face in front of everyone. It was embarrassing, degrading, and shaming.

As Jesus is talking, it's likely everybody is thinking about a time when they were insulted or slapped or offended by someone. John Ortberg has spoken and written on the subject of turning the other cheek; I once heard him describe it something like this. Jesus says, "Okay, now here's a scenario. Say you become my students. You're my disciples. Now you're living in a different kind of reality. You are living in a reality where your whole life and world is bathed by God's presence. Your honor doesn't come from people; it comes from God. You are living in a 'blessed are the poor in spirit' kind of reality. So if someone comes and hits you on the right cheek, now that you are receiving honor from the greatest being in the universe, you have some alternatives. Instead of fighting back or fleeing, just turn your face till you've got your left cheek jutting out there."[2] You can't backhand someone with your right hand on the left cheek. You'd have to really go for it, at which point you're no longer insulting the person; you're fighting the person. Again, in that culture, fighting someone means you're calling him your equal, not your servant.

Which is more courageous: to attack someone or to turn your cheek? I think when you turn your cheek and invite even more infliction, that requires more courage and has a degree of nobility that is unlike the world. Jesus is inviting the person who's been slapped on the cheek to reconcile this relationship in a way that is not violent, and in a way that is also not cowardly. It's a response to your enemy that requires great courage.

Give Your Tunic

Then Jesus says, "Okay, let's say someone wants to sue you and take your tunic." Everyone listening to Jesus also knows what this is. Think about this: if someone is being sued for his clothing, he must have absolutely nothing else to give. In Jesus' day, someone being sued for his tunic was usually a person who was in debt, someone who had nothing. It was usually a lender doing the suing. This guy owes the lender money so the lender goes after everything the borrower has. Now there's no such thing as pants in the Bible, which is interesting. You'll never read, "And Abraham put on his pants."

Men typically would have two or three tunics, and that would be what you would wash. It was like a muumuu—a man muumuu. Your tunic was like a dress that went all the way to your ankles. And then over that, you would wear a cloak. If you had no money, nothing left, someone you owed could sue you and take your tunic, which is a way of saying. "I have everything of yours." It's literally suing someone for his underwear. It was a way of shaming the person.

In Judaism, you were not allowed to sue for the cloak. It's against Levitical law because it puts the person in danger of freezing. So Jesus says, "Say someone takes you to court and sues you for your tunic. Right there in the court, right there with everyone looking, your enemy has already taken your tunic so you take off your cloak, as well, and hand it to him in front of everybody." He's asking people to stand there naked. Jesus is essentially telling his listeners, "Your honor comes from God, not from man." In Jesus' day nakedness is very shameful. Jesus is saying, "Just embrace that."

Imagine being the plaintiff, the lender. You're standing there and you're suing this man because you're angry with him.

You say, "Your Honor, I need his tunic. He owes me money." And the judge says, "Give him your tunic." The man gives you his tunic. Then the defendant says, "Take my cloak, as well." There he is, standing naked in the court before everyone. What would you feel like as the lender? Here is a man who has nothing; he's standing naked—in front of everybody! Ribs jutting out because he hasn't eaten in days. He tells you, "Now you have everything. You've taken everything from me."

What would you feel like as a plaintiff? You'd probably forgive his debt. You'd probably give him back his cloak. You'd likely even give him his tunic and say, "I'm sorry. I shouldn't have done this. I feel really bad about this. I can see you're struggling. Let's work this out." These are creative ways for disciples not to cower, not to flee, but also not to put up fists to attack and insult. It's a way to bring holy light to real darkness. It's a way to be salt and light to your enemies in a way that's truly powerful.

Jesus also tells us to go two miles if we are forced to go one. Here he's likely referring to the Roman soldiers who would often force people to carry their gear. There was no love lost for the "evil Romans" who occupied Israel. Surprisingly, Jesus encourages radical hospitality to the soldiers many felt were enemy occupiers. This act of doing even more than required sheds light on the unfairness of forced labor. In an age when most of the Jewish leaders were encouraging violence toward Roman soldiers, Jesus was encouraging heart-convicting hospitality.

Be an Advocate to Your Enemies

Sometimes it feels like you have too many adversaries. They get on your nerves or they say bad things to you. Sometimes they will send you an e-mail you weren't expecting. Sometimes at a party or at work they will insult you in front of your friends. Sometimes your employer will unfairly ask you to work on Saturday or Sunday or to stay late. And all of the time, we live in a world in which people shame us, put us down, dishonor us, and gossip about us.

But Jesus teaches us if we receive our honor from God and our whole purpose in life is to honor him, then those things, even though they hurt, don't matter as much because God wants us to be a part of healing the brokenness in that other person. He wants us to be an advocate for life, for peace, and for goodness. He's not asking us to be cowards; he's asking us to do the most creative and courageous thing we can possibly do. To turn the cheek. To give the cloak. To go the extra mile. That requires more courage than violence. It requires incredible nobility and strength.

Those of you who have done this in order to honor God and to do the right thing, you know what it feels like to turn your cheek, to take off your cloak and stand there in shame, and to go the extra mile. There is a great sense of God honoring you and blessing you. The martyr Stephen, when he gave his life, said, "Lord, do not hold this sin against them" (Acts 7:60). We have a sense that God is honoring us when we want to reconcile relationships more than we want to have our own way, to fight for our reputation, or to tell it like it is. God wants us to find new, creative ways to respond to our enemies.

By the way, the posture here is not to be self-righteous. This is not a new legalism. This is not saying, "I'm better than you. I'm taking the higher road than you." Rather, this is a holistic, pure desire to help reconcile this broken person with you and with God. There is great honor in that.

However, we want to be careful not to enter into abusive relationships. It's easy to think this passage means, "I need to be a doormat." That is not at all what Jesus wants for us. He simply wants us to reconcile with others. He wants us to be the first to say "I'm sorry" even though it isn't fair. Boundaries are important. Speaking the truth in love is important. Don't abandon that.

Christians destroy our enemies by making them our friends. We love our enemies. We love those who hate us. We care for the good of those who are violent toward us. We take no insult or offense when people persecute us or shame us or gossip about us or e-mail us or post about us on social media. We receive honor from God, and that's what it's all about.

You have heard that it was said, "Love your neighbor and hate your enemy." But I tell you, love your enemies and pray for those who persecute you, that you may be children of your Father in heaven. He causes his sun to rise on the evil and the good, and sends rain on the righteous and the unrighteous. If you love those who love you, what reward will you get? Are not even the tax collectors doing that? And if you greet only your own people, what are you doing more than others? Do not even pagans do that? Be perfect, therefore, as your heavenly Father is perfect.

—Matthew 5:43–48

9 Unstoppable Love

YOU THOUGHT I WAS DONE with loving your enemies, didn't you? This teaching is the heartbeat of the Sermon on the Mount, Jesus' great discourse on the kingdom of God. It is a summary of everything that the great Rabbi, Jesus, was teaching to his students. You can find 95 percent of everything Jesus believes in the Sermon on the Mount. So we need to give this "love your enemies" thing another chapter.

Loving your enemies is not a new law. For example, I do not believe Jesus is telling us to always turn the cheek when someone slaps us. Rather, he's telling us to think of creative, nonhostile ways to resolve things quickly with people who curse us.

I've had this method practiced on me by good people who responded to my contempt with patience and love. When I started seminary, I thought I knew everything. I began to openly criticize my systematic theology professor in front of the whole class, drawing dangerously close to calling him a heretic. I realized later that many of the things I said with indignation were outright false. The professor was kind. He simply listened, didn't really respond, and even took me out for pie the next week. He responded to my immaturity with patience and love, and he won me over as a protégé. This professor, Ray Anderson, was considered one of the brightest minds the seminary has ever had. He didn't use that against me. He could have humiliated me in front of everyone. Instead, he gained a passionate disciple.

Maybe you say, "Well, I don't really have any enemies." That's true for some people. I'm pretty sure Hannah, my wife, doesn't have any enemies. There are some people who genuinely do not have any enemies. But most of us have enemies in our lives.

If that's you, here is what I want you to think about instead of enemies. Think "competitors." Loving your enemies is essentially saying love everyone. And if you are to love your enemies, then it also means you're to love your competitors. It's easy for us to feel competitive with one another. Feeling jealousy toward someone means we have the opportunity to practice what Jesus teaches by blessing that person in some way. This can be a compliment, a gift, or a word of encouragement.

Jesus is telling you to love difficult people. It also means you have to be kind to yourself because sometimes your greatest enemy is you. People who are very harsh on themselves oftentimes treat others with that same harshness.

So when Jesus says to love your enemies, he's essentially saying to love everyone and do whatever you can to creatively resolve conflict. When people mess with your stuff. When people say nice things to your face and then e-mail things or text things behind your back. It means that if you're in business, academia, or in music, or in some kind of an industry where others want to see you fail, you instead want to see them thrive because you love them. This is the most difficult and most Christian thing about Jesus' teaching and, as we'll see in a minute, it's one of the most important things that sets us apart from our culture.

What makes you different from the average Joe on the street in the way you treat people? If you cannot come up with an honest answer to that question, then the assumption is that nothing does. And if nothing makes you different from the average Joe on the street, there's a problem.

We As God's Enemies

Loving our enemies is impossible until we understand God loved us when we were his enemies. There it is. You were God's enemy. I was God's enemy. I said things about him and hated him or denied him or hid my face from him and he still loved me. I hurt other people. I harmed his children. I lied and deceived, yet he still loved me and gave his Son for me.

When we talk about turning the cheek and about going the extra mile, think of it as "Jesus jujitsu." This is Dallas Willard's term.[1] Jujitsu is a martial art that uses your opponent's force against him- or herself. Jujitsu begins with discipline of the self and requires real training to focus the mind. You've seen jujitsu. It looks like Chinese or Japanese wrestling.

Think *Karate Kid*. We all know the scene where the guy goes to punch Mr. Miyagi, who sidesteps, and the guy punches his hand through the window. That's how Mr. Miyagi, an old frail man, takes down the Cobra Kai. He uses jujitsu.

Loving your enemies does not mean you cower and hide, or pretend to be nice, or respond by slapping back or retaliating. It means you create a third alternative, one where a person has to acknowledge and think about the fact that they've hurt you. They have to deal with it. That's what turning the cheek does.

The reason we need to be this way is because Jesus has a purpose for our lives, and that purpose is for us to be salt and light to others, to end the chain of violence that goes from one person to another, to refuse to pay back evil for evil. When you love your enemy, it affects your enemy in an incredible way. Using force works in the short run but never provides lasting results.

Being Made Whole

In Matthew 5, Jesus talks about loving your enemies. I want to begin examining the scripture with this one line. He says, "Be perfect, therefore, as your heavenly Father is perfect" (v. 48). Jesus looks at a group of people who are sick, angry, and poor—people who mess up all the time. There are Samaritans and lepers and prostitutes and tax collectors. Jesus looks at these people and says, "Be as perfect as God." Anybody else feel a little perplexed when you read this passage?

When we read "perfect," especially in our Western minds, we think it means "never sin or make a mistake." But that's not what this passage is saying. Jesus is not really saying, "Never sin, just as your Father never sins." The word we read as "perfect" is the Greek word *telios*. There is no English word for *telios*, so translators have struggled with this particular verse. *Telios* means "to be made whole or complete." There's a healing component to this word translated "perfect."

If a lad is, say, eleven years old, he's not *telios* until he's fully grown. When he's fully grown and in the prime of his life, he becomes *telios* or perfect. When a student graduates and receives his diploma, or when someone learns her discipline and masters it, that person is *telios*. They have perfected their studies. *Telios* comes from a similar word *telikos*, which means "end, purpose, aim, or goal." When you are *telios*, you have completely stepped into the thing you are made to do. Everything fits when you are *telios* because everything is made whole.

Once, I realized I had to really improve at running if I was going to win a particularly embarrassing contest. It was an abs competition, I'm ashamed to say. My chiropractor wanted me to do it. I was starting to get a little fat and felt like it would be good motivation. We all put fifty dollars in a pot and whoever had the best abs was going to win the pot. So, in order to train for this ridiculous contest, I realized I had to get into running.

I have a friend who's so into running it's like a drug. And he says, "If you want to get really good at running, we're going to go running ten miles every week. To do that, you need good shoes."

I said, "I have good shoes."

He said, "No, no, no, you need good shoes. You need shoes that fit."

"How much is this going to put me back?"

"About one hundred and fifty dollars."

"Whoa! I can't spend that much on shoes!"

The idea of spending all this money on shoes seemed wrong until I actually got the shoes. I went into an athletic store and the clerk said, "The first thing you're going to do is stick your feet in this gel." So I stuck my feet in the gel because each shoe has to match each foot perfectly. He took the gel imprint and input the information into a computer. Then I ran on a treadmill and he measured my feet and how much weight I placed on each foot. He went into the back and made a shoe for me. He brought out these shoes—the right shoe is made for my right foot, and the left shoe is made for my left foot. When my feet slip in, they're both just perfect. I can feel it when I run. It's as if the shoe is an extension of my foot.

Quite simply, my shoes were *telios*. Each one was perfect because they fit perfectly.

This is what Jesus means when he says, "Be perfect, therefore, as your heavenly Father is perfect." All of us have this missing puzzle piece. The shoe of our life doesn't seem to fit. Something is wrong, something is broken, something is out of place, and somehow we remain fractured, wounded, broken. Jesus says to be made whole! Be a completely whole person as your Father in heaven is completely whole.

Do you want to live this kind of life? I do. I want to be *telios*. Do you want to know how you can be *telios*? Jesus said it right before: "Love your enemies."

"Oh, maybe I don't want to be *telios*," you say. But great reward comes at great sacrifice and that is the Christian way. This is the very essence that Jesus was and is.

Revealing What God Is Like

When you read anything in Scripture and it says, "son of" something, it means the person is like something. For example, in Jesus' day, you might hear, "John, son of peace." That would mean that John is a very peaceful person. He's the essence of what it means to be peaceful. Or, "Joe, son of power." That meant that Joe is a very powerful person. This can be seen all over the Bible. Jesus says, "Love your enemies and pray for those who persecute you, so that you may be sons of your Father who is in heaven" (Matthew 5:44–45 ESV). He is saying that when you love your enemies, you are showing the world what God is like!

When you love your enemies, you reveal what kind of God our God is. That's what Jesus did. When Jesus came into the world, his purpose was to show us what God is like. So he loves the unloved, and he touches the untouchable. To eat with someone, in those days, was to call him or her your equal. Jesus would eat with prostitutes, tax collectors, sinners, pagans, and Roman soldiers. People in his day disqualified him as a prophet because he allowed himself to be in their company. People would say, "Rabbi, you're eating with this woman? Do you know who she is?" But Jesus gave his life willingly for them so they could be ultimately reconciled to God.

There is a passage in Luke where a woman of the night comes to Jesus weeping. She covers Jesus' feet in her tears and wipes his feet with her hair (Luke 7:36–50). Imagine that in my community there is a prostitute, and we all know who she is. One day, she comes running into the church and she gives me a big hug. In the church service, she starts crying. She weeps and hugs my feet. What is everybody going to be thinking? *What is going on here? What have these two been up to?*

Do you know what I would do as a pastor? My first temptation would be to say to her, "No, get away from me!" That's my wicked desire to manage my reputation. I want to protect the way people see me. I want my church to know that their pastor is clean. But that's not what Jesus did. In fact, he turned to the whole group with him and criticized them. He says in a roundabout way, "I came in here and you didn't wash my feet, and you didn't welcome me, and you didn't kiss me on the cheek, and here she's done this great act of worship." He honors her, welcomes her, and loves her in front of everybody.

Jesus reveals in his life what God is like. That is good news because, in the end, we're all like this woman. We're all broken, and we're all wounded. Some of us are just better than others at hiding it.

Think about the way that Jesus died. We all know Jesus died for us, but think about how he did it. At any moment, he could have raised a mob of followers to bring down the whole city of Jerusalem. Remember, Jesus had thousands and thousands of young men following him who would have taken up arms against the Romans at his request. Many of them desperately wanted to. Any moment he could have simply said the word. At any moment, he could have overcome the Romans in Jerusalem. But, no, he didn't. As Christians, we believe he also could have called down angels, fire, and thunder from the sky. Did he do it? No.

When Jesus was in the Garden of Gethsemane, he was betrayed by one of his closest friends. When the crowd came to arrest him, Peter, defending Jesus, drew his sword and cut off the ear of the high priest's slave. Jesus picked up the ear, placed it back on the man's head, turned to Peter, and said, "All who draw the sword will die by the sword" (Matthew 26:52).

On the cross Jesus said, "Father, forgive them for they don't know what they're doing" (Luke 23:34). You know, you can fake it only so much. When you're being whipped and beaten, bleeding and suffocating, you can't fake it anymore. Jesus wasn't posturing. Jesus actually loved the people who came to arrest him. Jesus even loved the Pharisees. Jesus loved his disciples who betrayed him in the moment of truth, because Jesus loves his enemies and Jesus reveals to us what God is like. Jesus is the Son of God. And Jesus tells us that we, too, can be sons and daughters of God—meaning if we are students of Jesus' way, we can reveal to the world what God is like. He's not a vindictive, angry, mean, lightning-throwing Zeus. God loves us and wants us to be reconciled. So, when we were his enemies, God loved us and he changed us so that we could love our enemies, so that we can help transform them.

Released from Bitterness

Jesus says, "If you love those who love you, what reward will you get? Are not even the tax collectors doing that? And if you greet only your own people, what are you doing more than others? Do not even pagans do that?" (Matthew 5:46–47). I might as well say, if you only love those who love you, do not even terrorists do that?

So what makes the manner and the posture that you have toward your neighbor who hates you, or your competitor, or that difficult person, different? As a person who's supposed to reveal what Jesus is like, what makes you different? As a believer how does your posture toward your neighbor stand out in the moment of truth so that people look and say, "Wow, John is different," "Wow, Sarah is different in the way she treats her colleagues"? People notice that when that person says a horrible thing about you, about your school, about your workplace, about your parents, or about your spouse or child, you are so different in your maturity and your love for your neighbor. There is something divine about you.

This concept of loving our enemies can be confusing, because when we use the word *love* we particularly think about an emotion. "I can't have warm, fuzzy feelings toward my enemies," we say. I'm happy to tell you that loving is not about having particular emotions toward your neighbor.

The word for love Jesus uses is *agapao*, or *agape*. It's a God kind of love, a love that never ends. It specifically means "care for human good." It means that you can dislike someone and still genuinely love him or her. The idea is that you want the best for that person even when they harm you and your loved ones.

I remember a pastor who taught very poorly on this subject. When he taught this passage in the Sermon on the Mount about turning the cheek, he gave this example. There was some rude guy he wanted to fight and his mentor said, "Don't worry, son. Someday he'll get his own." So gritting his teeth, the pastor passed on fighting this unsavory guy. Then with joy, he told the congregation, "I found out two months later that he picked a fight with somebody else and got the tar beat out of him." Everybody laughed and clapped.

That is not the kind of heart Jesus is talking about. Jesus is saying that, although you want justice, although you may feel frustrated, even angry, you don't allow bitterness, vengeance, or especially contempt, a cold posture toward your neighbor, to ever creep into your heart. You wouldn't want that person to get in a fight a month from now, so that you can have vengeance. You want that person to become a good person. You see your own woundedness, anger, and brokenness reflected back at you from the person who's insulting or gossiping about you. And you think about how God changed you and rescued you. When you were God's enemy, he gave his Son for you. And you see the person who is your enemy and you say, "I want that for him too." That is what a mature Christ-follower looks like.

When you allow your unforgiveness and bitterness toward your enemies (or your competitors) to fester, they win! Friends, *they* win. You may have enemies who have been nemeses for a long, hard time, and the older you get, I'm sure the more you have. Those of you who have enemies and people you feel hatred toward in your heart, they have a power over you. Even after they die, they'll still have that power over you. They likely relish in your woundedness and want you to feel this way. They celebrate in your pain. Yet when will forgive and even love your enemy, you are released from that power.

A Radical, Loving Response to Enemies

So we're supposed to love our enemies, which means we're supposed to care for their good. That means we're supposed to do radical things. When we get bad service at a restaurant, we leave a huge tip. Bad service is a pet peeve of mine. One time I got such horrible service, I left a penny. I left a penny because I didn't want him to think that I forgot to tip. I wanted him to know that his service was worth about a penny. See, that's Bobby Schuller. That's what Bobby Schuller is like. And Bobby Schuller died. He was crucified, and now Bobby Schuller doesn't live, but Christ lives in him. So what do I do now when I get bad service? First, we shouldn't care that much about getting good service. We should just let it go. Second, we should leave a huge tip; huge, like 40 or 50 percent, and write a kind note on the receipt. We're Christians, friends! We're supposed to be different.

Someone's going to say something bad to you or gossip about you behind your back. Instead of doing the same, look for the best in that person and tell everybody about how great he or she is. We are Christians, friends. We're supposed to be different. When you hear gossip about what somebody has said about you, go straight to that person. Do not relish or gossip back. Do not triangulate. We are Christians. We're supposed to be different. Love your enemies. Pray for your competitors. Pray for difficult people.

Every time someone crosses a line you have an opportunity to be radical in your love. And this will happen. Someone will say something rude to you, someone will cut you off in traffic, someone will give you bad service at a restaurant, someone will cross some boundaries or bother you, and you are going to have another opportunity. Your opportunity is to show this person what God is like, a God who loves his enemies, and we can rejoice in that. We can know that no matter what we have, what we do, what people say about us, God loves us and he wants us and he believes in us. We then can reciprocate that to our neighbor.

That is what it means to be like Jesus, to love our enemies. It means to be a change agent, to be salt and light to a hurting and broken world. Your enemy does not need a curse. He does not need someone to say something bad about him. He needs someone to bless him, to love him, and to encourage him. If we don't change things, no one else is going to. It's going to happen one person at a time, one blessing at a time, one relationship at a time, one cubicle to the next, one phone to the other, one e-mail to another. We have the opportunity today and every day, to show someone what God is really like. God loves his enemies. Praise God!

• •

Be careful not to practice your righteousness in front of others to be seen by them. If you do, you will have no reward from your Father in heaven.

So when you give to the needy, do not announce it with trumpets, as the hypocrites do in the synagogues and on the streets, to be honored by others. Truly I tell you, they have received their reward in full. But when you give to the needy, do not let your left hand know what your right hand is doing, so that your giving may be in secret. Then your Father, who sees what is done in secret, will reward you.

—Matthew 6:1–4

• •

10 Secretly Good

S O FAR IN THE SERMON ON THE MOUNT, Jesus has talked about conquering anger, conquering lust, conquering lying, becoming a person who genuinely loves one's enemies, and becoming *telios*. Next he will speak to those who are saying, "I am doing all these things. I don't lie anymore, I have no anger or contempt in my heart, I don't lust anymore, I love my enemies, and I tell the truth." Finally he speaks to the person who says, "I have already conquered those things. Aren't you proud of me?"

Vainglory is a secret sin. It's the thing that only you're doing. Nobody else around you knows. It's a spiritual sin. It's a secret thing between you and God. It's when you're trying to manage the way you look, manage your achievements, your religious duty, and your good deeds. You subtly want people to know these good attributes about you. Once you allow that thing into yourself, you've crossed a dangerous line because vainglory is very hard to see. *Vainglory is the only sin that also*

119

requires virtue. Vainglory means we've done something good, and doesn't that make us so great?

Each of us wants to be a good person. We want to do the right thing, but we shouldn't want to do it in order to be honored by others. If being honored by others is the most important thing then reputation becomes more important than true inner virtue.

When You Give . . .

Jesus did not say that everything you do has to be secret. It certainly can sound that way. Rather, the goal is simply not to care what others think. You do what is right because you love what is right.

In Matthew 6, Jesus says:

> Be careful not to practice your righteousness in front of others to be seen by them. If you do, you will have no reward from your Father in heaven.
>
> So when you give to the needy, do not announce it with trumpets, as the hypocrites do in the synagogues and on the streets, to be honored by others. Truly I tell you, they have received their reward in full. But when you give to the needy, do not let your left hand know what your right hand is doing, so that your giving may be in secret. Then your Father, who sees what is done in secret, will reward you. (vv. 1–4)

Remember, Jesus' audience is very poor. Yet he says to these people three times in four verses, "When you give." *When you give?* He's not just telling them to give. He is assuming that every single person there is already giving because that's what disciples do. His followers give and it doesn't matter how poor or how rich they are. Jesus believes that a giving person is living in a different reality, with a dependence on God. A giving person cares more about others than about him- or herself.

Jewish tradition has a wonderful and well-developed theology of giving and charity. In fact, the Hebrew word for "almsgiving" is the same word as "justice" and "righteousness": *tzedakha*. It's presumed in Judaism that giving to charities, or giving to those in need, is the same as righteousness or any other justice issue.

Jesus is saying, "The hypocrites give just like you all give, but they're hypocrites because they sound the trumpets." Now what is he talking about there? Jesus coined the term *hypocrite* as it's currently used. It was a word that already existed but it simply meant "actor." It wasn't a pejorative term when Jesus first started using it. It would be as if you went to a play tonight and you got the playbill, and it said hypocrite one, hypocrite two, hypocrite three. That would be three actors.

Jesus is saying that secretly, these people are different than you think they are. They're actors. It would be as if there was some guy onstage at our church doing something really holy and I came up and said, "And the Oscar goes to . . ." Jesus is saying these are people who wear masks. They're pretending to be righteous, they're pretending to care for the poor, they're pretending to be generous and to be living in the kingdom of God, but that's all they're doing. They're pretending. They're doing it in order to get people to give them glory. Well, that's exactly what they're going to get. They're going to get the reward of people applauding them for about fifteen seconds, and that's all they're going to get.

When we see this blowing of the trumpets, we picture people hearing the sound and someone saying, "Everyone gather around." But that's not what happened in Jesus' day. The shofar would come out, blow for the feasts and the holy ceremonies, and then everyone would come to the temple. Some people who had their gift to give would give it quietly at any time in a little box near the door. In contrast, instead of just giving it anytime, the hypocrites would hold on to it, stand by, and wait for the horn to be blown. They'd specifically time it so that when the crowds started to come, they'd walk in, say hi to their friends, and when everyone was looking, they'd drop their gift into the box. They timed their gift because they didn't genuinely care about what God thought. They may not have even cared about helping others. What they cared most about was managing their religious reputation. They cared only about what other people thought. They wanted others to know they were in good religious standing with the temple.

There may have been some other guy who gave a donation at the same time. He may have given when the trumpets were sounding, but he was not timing it. He didn't care. He just happened to be there and that's okay. Jesus is talking about this person who times it for the entire world to see.

Take Off Religious Masks

This timing, this wanting to do good things in front of others, just dropping in, it's a secret thing. People don't know that these guys who are timing were sitting there for an hour and a half waiting for the shofar to be blown so everyone could see them give their money.

We do this kind of thing all the time. Think about the way we subtly drop names of friends, the way we accidentally leave our charity envelopes on the kitchen counter when our friends come over. The way we happen to mention that we can't make it because we're going to be serving at the soup kitchen tonight.

I constantly struggle with this. All pastors are tempted to manage their religious masks. Sometimes the reason I push some boundaries when I preach, even about things pastors are supposed to and not supposed to say, is because I'm trying to break free from needing approval from others. I know I do it all the time.

I go to Rancho Capistrano every Friday and I pray. I slate it as uninterruptable time. I spend the whole day there in silence, solitude, and praying for the people I love. Now when I can't make it to a meeting on Friday, I could simply say I have an appointment on Friday. But what I usually do is say, "I'm sorry, I can't make it. I'll be praying all day." I just realized that I do this. When I do this, I am seriously trying to let people know that prayer is an important part of my life as a pastor, that this part of my spiritual life is covered, and they don't have to worry about it. But when I do this I am focusing more on honor from people than from God.

Care about What God Thinks

We are compelled to manage our reputations. We do it with our clothes, with our house, and with our highlighted Bibles. We give and tell people we gave because we desire the reward of their approval more than God's approval.

Dan Allender talks about a time when he went to his daughter's piano recital and all the parents were there. His daughter, halfway through her song, froze. She couldn't go on, and she was just staring at the piano. A number of heads turned and looked at Dan, who was watching her. He was thinking that everybody thought he didn't train her well enough, or didn't give her good enough lessons, or she didn't practice enough. There was a tension in the room.

She started playing again and the tension went down until the audience realized that she didn't continue; she started over. So the tension started to build as she got closer and closer to the point where she couldn't remember the song. When she got to that point, she froze again. At the piano, she turned to the audience and just shrugged her shoulders. A little eight-year-old girl. Dan said he was mortified. Everybody was looking at him as the piano teacher came up and gave his daughter the music and then she continued playing.

Dan said, "We're at this horrible event. I'm in the seventh circle of hell, and we all have these cookies the piano teacher seemed to have bought in ton blocks. They're disgusting and there's this pink liquid that's supposed to be reminiscent of lemonade but is actually carcinogenic. All the parents are talking and congratulating each other on how well their children did." He recounted how people came up to him including one guy who actually said, "Your daughter shrugged well."

Afterward, Dan walked out to his car in front of his wife and his daughter, happy to get out of there. As he got closer to the car, his eight-year-old daughter pulled at his jacket and said, "Daddy, why do you hate me?"

"I don't hate you, darling."

"Well, then, why haven't you talked to me? Why haven't you looked at me? Why haven't you touched me?"

He then realized that he was more concerned about what people thought about him as a parent than about his own child. He was trying to appear educated and a great parent with great kids. "I wounded deeply my daughter with my own selfishness and vainglory."[1]

We do this all the time! We want people to see how great we are, all the things we've achieved. It's like a child who plants something in the soil, watches it start to grow, and when a little green shoot comes up, this is our good works. Then all of a sudden we reach down, pluck it out of the ground, and say, "Look what I got!" That's what showing off your religious goodness is like. By showing it off to others, we assure it will never take root, it will never bear fruit, and it is worth nothing.

Those men who gave to be seen by others got their reward in full. They got the congratulations and the approval of their neighbor. But God had a greater reward for them. Something so awesome, a tremendous reward they would have received, but now they will get nothing except for the fifteen seconds of approval from their neighbor. Jesus says there is a much greater reward for those who give in a discreet way.

They genuinely love God and people, and they frankly don't want any credit from others. They themselves have already received so much from the Lord, and from their neighbor. Giving secretly, then, is a discipline that proves you care about your neighbor and you care about what God thinks. Giving secretly diminishes our selfishness.

The Secret You Is the Real You

Jesus finishes this passage by saying, "Then your Father, who sees what is done in secret, will reward you" (Matthew 6:4). I want you to pay attention to this word *secret*. Secret stuff is the best. The most remarkable, interesting, and coolest things are secret stuff.

Jonah Berger gives us a great example of this in his book *Contagious*. Somewhere in New York City, there is a small hot dog place called Crif Dogs. It's nondescript, a little joint with a small sign over the door. You go into Crif Dogs and order a delicious hot dog. You're sitting there, eating a hot dog, when you look in the corner and see an antique phone booth and it strikes your fancy. You think, *Oh, that's interesting*. It's one of those phone booths like in the old Superman movies where Clark Kent enters, closes the door, and when he exits, he has turned into Superman!

So you walk over and sit down in the phone booth. You close the door and put the phone to your ear. It's a turn dial, so you turn it to number two. A voice comes on and says, "Do you have a reservation?" You have no idea what this is, so you say, "No I don't have a reservation." And the voice says, "Well, you're in luck. We have one opening. Would you like to use it?" And you say, "Yes." You don't know what's going to happen.

You hang up the phone and all of a sudden, the wall where the phone hangs opens up to a secret stairway. You walk down this stairway into an old cellar that's been transformed into this killer bar. The name of the bar is Please Don't Tell. This is a real bar and it is the hottest bar in New York. It isn't easy to get a reservation for Please Don't Tell; they open reservations at 3:00 every afternoon and by 3:15 every reservation is taken for the rest of the evening. They don't advertise; they don't tell anybody about it. The whole purpose is to have a secret, hidden bar. There's something special about secret stuff, isn't there?[2]

If you tell someone, "I have to tell you something. This is a secret," then it's been proven that the person is more likely to share your information.

Anytime you do something in secret, whether it's good or bad, it's like it's on steroids. If you do something good and you don't tell anybody about it, and later they find out you did this great thing in secret, everybody thinks, *Wow! You're such a hero*! If you do something really dark and wicked, you do it secretly, and people find out about it, they think, *Oh man, you're a villain. You are just a really bad person.*

Think of all the stories and movies in which there's a man and a woman and they're not getting along very well. The man seems mean and crude, and she hates him. But then she looks into his life. She finds out that this guy secretly loves her and secretly does all these great things for people and has been secretly helping her family. He's now different somehow and she finds herself falling in love. Mr. Darcy in *Pride and Prejudice* was like that.

When someone says something about you secretly, it's truer than what they say about you publicly. If I say something about our friend Joe while Joe is present, but then I pull you to the side and I say something else about Joe that's different, which comment is going to be true? When you say things about people in secret, that's the most true something can be. Secrecy is an important part of our spiritual life.

The secret you is the real you. And that's the part God wants to change. He doesn't care about your pretending. He doesn't care about your clothing or your material goods. He does not care about what others think or say about you. He doesn't care if others think you're religious or a good person. He cares about who you actually are in secret. He wants to make you secretly good. He wants to make you a person with no skeletons in your closets. Jesus wants to change the secret you and make you secretly good.

God Secretly Loves You

Would you rather be an evil man that everybody thought good or a good man that everybody thought evil? If you had to choose, if everybody in the world thought you were evil but you're actually good, or if everybody in the world thought you were a saint but you're really a bad person—which would you choose? I think everybody knows the right answer. But honestly, ask yourself, what does your heart say? What would you actually want?

We do all these things in public to hide the way we are secretly. But God wants to switch that around. God secretly loves you. God—who dwells in an invisible place with power enough to create or destroy the entire universe, who cradles your soul in the palm of his hand with joy and adores you as a mother adores her new baby—this God secretly loves you. The knowledge of God's love must be a deep, inner secret knowledge of God's deep and abiding love for you in the most secret and darkest places of your heart. The knowledge of God's love dwelling there is the antidote for vainglory. It is the thing that says, "I don't care if people see or don't see my works. I don't care about my reputation any longer. I'm not what I do. I'm not what I have. I'm not what people say about me. I'm a child of God, and that's the only thing that matters."[3]

People will say all sorts of things about you. But there's nothing you can do to lose God's love. You didn't earn it, and you're never going to lose it. If you can really imbed that truth in the secret part of your life, that knowledge will change you forever. Give, do good things, bless others, but abandon vainglory. Be a humble, gentle disciple and student of Jesus.

• •

This, then, is how you should pray:

"Our Father in heaven,
hallowed be your name,
your kingdom come,
your will be done,
    on earth as it is in heaven.
Give us today our daily bread.
And forgive us our debts,
    as we also have forgiven our debtors.
And lead us not into temptation,
    but deliver us from the evil one."

For if you forgive other people when they sin against you, your heavenly Father will also forgive you. But if you do not forgive others their sins, your Father will not forgive your sins.

—Matthew 6:9–15

• •

11 Prayer Is Letting Go

HAVE YOU EVER broken a promise? I have.

I broke a promise to myself that I wouldn't fly a certain airline. They had lost my bags several times. I'd found myself stuck on a tarmac for hours with no air conditioning. So I promised myself I would never fly this particular airline ever again. I'd always tell people, "Don't ever put me on this airline if you're going to fly me somewhere." One time those booking my ticket didn't get the message, purchased a ticket for me on this particular airline, and I acquiesced. I would soon regret it.

I was coming back from Dallas to Orange County with my wife, and it was a fine flight. I was amazed. Up to this point, we actually took off on time, the air-conditioning worked, and we were about to descend into Orange County. Yet I noticed we were still pretty high, and we flew right over Orange County airport. *Hmm.* We were still pretty high—now all I could see was just ocean and more ocean. Twenty minutes later, I was thinking, *Are we on our way to Hawaii? What's going on here?* My wife and I were sitting there confused.

Have you ever heard the voice of a pilot when he's a little shaken? It's not a comforting feeling. Our pilot came on the loudspeaker and said, "Ladies and gentlemen, the flaps on the side of the plane are not operating. We can turn the plane, but we can't slow it down. We're going to perform an emergency landing at LAX because it has a long enough runway. This will be a highly dangerous emergency crash landing." (I'm not sure how much of this was actually said but that's the gist of what I heard.)

The flight attendants were freaking out. That never happens. Usually the flight attendants act like, "It's no big deal. Been there, done that." These flight attendants were more like, "Seat belts on! Seat belts on! Heads down! You will keep your heads down at all times!" We all had our heads in our laps like we were kissing our knees. And the whole time I was thinking, *Of course, the one time I break my promise not to fly this horrible airline, and this is what happens.*

We approached LAX going really fast, and as we got close to the ground, I peeked out the window. I've never seen buildings going by so fast. The flight attendants were shouting at the passengers, "Heads down! Heads down!" Mine was one of those heads that was not all the way down; I was peeking a little. As we came close, I looked out the window and saw a bunch of fire trucks and ambulances driving alongside the plane while it was still flying only a few feet above the runway.

Just before this, as we were getting close to landing, Hannah had grabbed my hand and said, "Let's pray." So we prayed. And after we prayed, she said, "Everything's going to be just fine. I have a peace." I have a feeling we weren't the only ones praying on that plane. One of the funny things about that experience was how calm everybody was. I was surprised by that. I always thought, in an experience like that, people would be freaking out. Yet everybody was very stoic and calm. I knew there were people on that plane who were praying who don't normally pray.

As we came close to the runway, the pilot did this special maneuver. My grandpa Kerry, who's a pilot, explained this maneuver to me. We came down, the wheels barely touched the runway, and then the airplane went back into flight only a few feet off the ground. So we flew over the runway for another minute or so. I couldn't believe how long the runway was. The plane touched down gently again and then went back in the air, still flying. Essentially that's what they were doing to slow down the plane. Then the third or fourth time, it was a nice, smooth landing. If the pilot hadn't said anything, we might not have known there was an emergency landing at all. Grandpa Kerry said it was actually a very dangerous situation. But we landed and everything was fine.

The pilot then shared that we had a choice—switch planes and fly to Orange County or we could drive about forty-five minutes to Orange County. I'm not sure anyone took the flying option.

The funniest thing about the experience was that when the plane finally came to a stop, you could feel the tension drop in everyone on the plane. One passenger said aloud, "It's good to be alive!" And everybody shouted, "Yeah!" It was a great feeling.

Prayer is a natural thing people do in situations like that. I have often thought that prayer didn't come out of religion, but religion came out of prayer. There are times when we're in situations like on that plane, that even those without any religious background would pray, "If somebody's up there, please help me out here. I don't want to die." Life is good, right? There is something about human beings, particularly when things get bad, that makes us want to turn our eyes heavenward and pray to something or someone.

The message I want to give you is this: don't wait until you're in an emergency to pray. That's what most of us do. We come to God and we come into the life of prayer only when things get bad. That is not the way disciples are meant to live. Of course, you go to God in prayer when things are bad. Yes, you should do that, but don't wait until then. Prayer is so good. It should be used every day.

What Is Prayer?

If I were to simplify the concept of prayer, I would say, *prayer is letting go*. Not letting go in the sense of "I quit," but letting go in the sense of "I know if I release this thing to God, everything will turn out better in the long run." Prayer is letting go. Now in other religions, that is certainly not the case. If you look at other religions, many view God or the gods as wrathful, angry, vengeful, and temperamental deities that are just out to get us. Some people have this false view of God in Christianity.

Prayer in some of these other religions will create ways we can appease the gods in the hopes they'll hear our cry.

Though this concept has certainly leaked into Christianity at times, it does not reflect how Christians should pray. Praying, for a Christian, does not mean asking yourself:

What can I do to influence God's decision-making process?

How can I be in a more sacred space?

How can I sacrifice my money or time to get God to hear me better?

How can I get superspiritual people to pray for me since God will probably listen to them?

That's not how Christians pray.

Christianity says prayer is essentially letting go. When we pray, whether we're asking God for something or we're asking for forgiveness or for help or for guidance or for insight, prayer is essentially saying to God, "Not my will but yours be done." At its core, Christian prayer sounds like, "God, I am troubled by this, but I release it to you." And you know what? Christians have every reason to let go to God because God is a good God who loves us.

We're like a kid who is dangling from the roof, and the dad says, "Just let go. I'll catch you!"

And we say, "No!"

He says, "Just let go. I'll catch you."

God is good, we can trust him, and we can pray to him. There really isn't a right or wrong way to pray. In fact, the crux of the Sermon on the Mount and the Lord's Prayer is essentially saying that you need to stop trying to manipulate God or influence God. Prayer is letting go.

Prayer is, for the Christian, the greatest source of power and grace. It's what energizes us and gives us fuel to be a Jesus kind of person. Through prayer we realize we can't do life on our own. It gives us an incredible power to say to God very simply, "I am wounded. I am broken. I am a sinner. I am lost, I need you, I can't do this on my own, and I need your help."

God Is Always Around

Prayer is the way in which we recognize that God doesn't go anywhere. When we pray, we don't ask God to be a part of our life. Rather, when we pray, we're acknowledging that he's right there with us, that he's been with us since we were born, and that he's listening.

God is always around, and this is important. When I was a kid I used to imagine what it would be like if my dad was always around. My dad is super cool. I remember when I was a kid he loved to go fishing, and not on Saturdays when I didn't have school. He loved to go fishing on weekdays. On the days he would go fishing, he would take me to school first. I'd be there for a couple of hours. I was in third or fourth grade. I just didn't want to be there. I had to do math or some other boring subject. All of a sudden, a kid would come in with a note, the teacher would look up at the class, and everybody would think, *Who gets to leave?* She'd say, "Bobby Schuller." Yes! *There's Dad.* The first time he did that, I asked him, "What's wrong?" Dad said, "What's wrong is that we have a boat and it doesn't have fish in it. We're going fishing."

I think for a kid, there's something about having your dad around that makes things easier. If you were bullied at school or had kids picking on you, they wouldn't do it if your dad was around. As a kid, if your dad is around, you don't have to worry about anything because you know your dad will take care of it. For the Christian, in a spiritual sense, knowing God is around creates this childlike sense to release your life in trust to him. It's like kids trusting that their loving parents will give them the food they need, will take them to the places they need to go, and will protect them from scary kids. This trust will help them push on through challenges and will teach them when they don't have answers to difficult questions.

That's what prayer does. It turns our ear to the voice of God and turns our body to the presence of God. It reminds us that God is always there and will never leave us. It keeps the memory of his love deep in our hearts, reminding us that he has a plan for us. For everything we're going through, no matter how bad, he has a plan to overcome it for good. Therefore, prayer is a necessity in the disciples' ability to live like Jesus. Loving your enemies, not being an angry person, not lying or managing your reputation, not worrying—that stuff is impossible without the inner life of prayer.

A Life Saturated with Prayer

Prayer must be our daily sustenance. Even Jesus, the Son of God, needed to pray. Jesus' ministry begins with his baptism. At this sacred event God lavishes him with love and favor, even though he hasn't really done anything yet in the story. Out of that place of God's love and goodness, Jesus then goes into the wilderness to be alone with the Father for forty days. There the devil tempts him but God's presence is made true and felt through the Scriptures. We constantly see Jesus withdrawing to be in prayer, to know that the Father is with him and that the Father has called him to receive guidance. If Jesus needed prayer, I know I do too.

So the Christian life is a life that should be saturated with prayer. Your life should be covered in prayer—praying when you get up, praying before your meals, praying for your friends when they share the disappointments and suffering of their lives. We should pray before meetings, pray before social gatherings, and yes, even pray when we fly.

If every Christian had a twenty-minute quiet time every morning, the whole world would be different. How different would your life be if you took twenty minutes every morning to be in a secret, special, beautiful place with God, praying and listening to him? Imagine your day starting in the presence of God, his presence washing over you. Over the years, how different would your life be? I think most of us know that if we took just twenty minutes every morning to spend some time praying and listening and reflecting, our lives would be totally different.

Keep that point in mind while I ask another question. What's more important to you: God or money? Many of us would say with absolute assurance that God is more important than money. Unfortunately, this is not actually true for most of us. You say, "My relationship with God would take on new life and power if I would spend twenty minutes with him every morning, but I just can't make the time to do that." What if I told you I would give you ten million dollars in a briefcase if you have a twenty-minute quiet time every morning for one year, but you can't miss even once? How many of you would do that? All of us would likely make time for a quiet time every day, never missing for a year, because of the money. We'd be insane not to. Yet it also means growing in faith is not as important to us as getting lots of money.

Now I'm talking to myself here because I try to have a quiet time every morning and I don't. I think I would do it if there were money involved, or I would do it if there were some kind of material reward. And that gives us a clue into where we are, and again, how much we need prayer. I don't say that to condemn you or make you feel shame, except to say that you may not love God as much as you think.

Admitting We Need Help

Praying every morning and setting aside time to be with God is admitting to God that you can't do your life on your own. When you stop every single morning and for fifteen, twenty, thirty minutes, an hour, you just say, "God, I can't do today without you," you are saying that you yield your life to God. That's where all power comes for Christians. We don't win through willpower and through trying harder. Christians have all power by having communion with the Father.

It's kind of like Alcoholics Anonymous because they encourage members to say, "I am broken, and I have no power to overcome this horrible thing in my life." The first step in AA or any of the addiction support groups is simply to abandon your ability to control your life to a higher power. Those in recovery are more in touch with their wounds and helplessness than most Christians. This allows them to inherit a deeper life with God, based not on personal willpower but power from outside themselves, the power that comes from the Holy Spirit. Yet all of us are broken and all of us need God, none more or less than another.

So prayer is a rhythm in which we say, "God, I need you. God, I let go." If we don't have a life of prayer, we essentially believe we don't need God in the ways the Bible says we do. Students go to class, athletes go to the gym, and Christians go to the prayer room. That's what we do. You cannot be a true disciple of Christ without a daily, ongoing life of prayer.

A life of prayer will bring such fullness and richness to your job that the job you hate will become a job you like (or at least can endure). Your marriage may be struggling, and then you'll love your spouse more. Your kids won't be a burden to you; they'll be a blessing to you. You'll start treating your neighbor with dignity and respect. But it doesn't happen overnight. You'll see the changes over the months by taking some time each day to be with Jesus. It will change your life.

How to Pray

You may be asking, "Well then, how do I pray?" This brings us to the Sermon on the Mount.

When Jesus begins the Sermon on the Mount, he says, "When you pray, do not be like the hypocrites, for they love to pray standing in the synagogues and on the street corners to be seen by others. Truly I tell you, they have received their reward in full. But when you pray, go into your room, close the door and pray to your Father, who is unseen. Then your Father, who sees what is done in secret, will reward you" (Matthew 6:5–6).

Jesus is talking about the religious guys like me, the pastors of the day who used to get in front of everyone and pray this great, eloquent prayer to show how spiritual they are. And Jesus said, "No, no, no, don't be like them. You don't need to show off your spirituality. People don't need to see you praying. In fact, what I want you to do is to go to a very secret place because that's where God is. Then your Father, who lives in a secret place, will hear your prayer."

Go to a Secret Place

The first thing we learn from the Sermon on the Mount is that when we pray, we ought to go to a very secret place. I think we ought to go to a secret, and if possible, beautiful place. Go someplace where God feels real to you. When that happens, when you're there, you get to be your real self. You get to talk about all of your stuff to God, and he'll meet you there.

Don't Babble

Then Jesus says, "And when you pray, do not keep on babbling like pagans, for they think they will be heard because of their many words. Do not be like them, for your Father knows what you need before you ask him" (Matthew 6:7–8). Have you ever seen Christians who babble on like pagans when they pray? In pagan prayers from the Roman Empire, the pagans would list every god they could think of—Zeus, Athena, Neptune, and so on—hoping that one of them would hear the heartfelt prayer.

I think probably, in Jesus' day, there were many Jewish pastors who would put a lot of thought into making the perfect prayer. So religious people would want to get their prayers just right, increasing their odds of a positive divine answer. "I want to get it right, and I want it to be a long prayer, and in-depth because then maybe God will hear me." Jesus says not to worry about it. When you pray, don't worry about doing it right. Don't worry about saying the right things.

I get all sorts of questions, like "Do I pray to Jesus or do I pray to the Father?" It's whichever one you want.

"When I pray, do I need to say in the name of the Father, Son, and Holy Spirit?"

"Do I need to do it in the name of Jesus?"

Those are all good things. Do them, but just stop worrying about it. Just go and be with God and say, "Lord, I'm here. Help. I'm letting go."

The Lord's Prayer

Next, Jesus gives us a model prayer. In the Sermon on the Mount, he says, "This, then, is how you should pray" (Matthew 6:9).

"Our Father . . ." (v. 9). That could be its own sermon when he says "Our Father." This is first-person plural. He doesn't say, "My Father." Anytime you pray the Lord's Prayer, you're praying in community with all Christians, even if you're completely alone. By saying "Our Father," you recognize that everyone who's praying this prayer is your brother and sister. It's also amazing Jesus doesn't say, "Our God." But he says, "Our Dad," "Our Father," "Our Abba." That was fresh. He

essentially begins by saying, "God, you're our dad. *Our* dad."
When you say it like that, it changes it to the loving Father
of many.

"*. . . in heaven*" (v. 9). This is the most misunderstood part
of the Lord's Prayer. The word "heaven" there is actually plural, "the heavens." It should say, "Who fills the heavens." This
is important because it shows us the "heaven" Jesus is talking
about is not just the one we go to when we die. Heaven, when
plural like this, means the sky, the stars, and the planets, and
even air around us. So when Jesus said, "Our Father who art
in the heavens," he's referring to the physical space around us.
God literally fills the whole universe and the space around us.

"*Hallowed be your name*" (v. 9). He essentially says, "We
treasure and value your name."

"*Your kingdom come, your will be done, on earth as it is
in heaven*" (v. 10). That essentially says, "I want you to be the
king of my life. I want everything that you want in my life."

"*Give us today our daily bread*" (v. 11). That means, "Give
us what we need." Again, there's the plural "us" form. When
you say in your prayer, "Give us today our daily bread," you're
essentially saying, "I want you to give my neighbor his daily
bread, and I want you to give me my daily bread. Give *us all*
what we need."

"*Forgive us our debts, as we also have forgiven our debtors*"
(v. 12). Here's the most incredible part of the Lord's Prayer.
Are you ready to say that, really? When we ask God to forgive
us our debts as we forgive our debtors, we are saying, "Forgive
us *to the same degree* we have forgiven those who have hurt
us." Think of the person you have forgiven the least in your

life. When you say, "Forgive us our debts, as we also have for-given our debtors," you are asking God to forgive you to the degree that you have forgiven that person.

At the end of this passage, Jesus says, "For if you forgive other people when they sin against you, your heavenly Father will also forgive you. But if you do not forgive others their sins, your Father will not forgive your sins" (vv. 14–15). Think about that. We are saying to God when we pray this, "God, I am so good at forgiving people that I'm asking you to forgive me to the same degree."

I got to practice this yesterday. I go to Disneyland all the time. And I was in the process of finding a parking space at downtown Disney, and my daughter had to use the restroom. She's four years old and potty trained, but she could still have an accident. She said, "Daddy, I have to go potty. I have to go real bad!" I knew I had about a minute or two, and then she was going to go no matter what. And all the parking spots were filled.

There was a woman walking to her car, and I was driving alongside her. I followed her until she got to her car because I needed to park right away. I put my blinker on, and she pulled out. My daughter was going crazy because she had to go potty, and I was in a hurry because otherwise she's going to go in the car. Then this car pulled out in a way that it blocked me and allowed another car to pull in. I had followed her all the way at a snail's pace, all the way through the parking lot. I was so angry. Later I realized it was trivial; it wasn't a big deal, but it took me a while. I was fighting myself. Those are the times when you can see how much you've grown in Christ. Now what does a Christian do? We acknowledge our anger and frustration at the selfishness of this person, but still, we let it go. I didn't do that. After finally finding another parking spot I rushed to get my daughter to the bathroom and thought about it the rest of the time at the park. When I pray, "Forgive us our debts," I'm asking God to forgive me to the degree that I forgave that woman who took my parking spot.

"Lead us not into temptation but deliver us from the evil one" (v. 13). We often say, "Deliver us from evil." But Jesus said, "Deliver us from the evil one." That refers either to the devil or to evil people in your life.

Praying Simply

The Lord's Prayer is so simple. It's essentially saying, "You're our Dad. You love us, and you're here with us. We treasure, value, and worship your name, and we can't do anything without you. We simply ask you to give us, today, everything we need. Forgive us of our sins as we forgive all of those around us and continue to forgive them. And help us to lead good and righteous lives." You see, Jesus doesn't want us to worry about praying perfectly. He wants us to pray simply.

Years ago at one of the churches I was a part of, there was a rumor the pastor would pray three hours every morning. I remember thinking, *How could you pray three hours in one morning?* My problem was I viewed prayer only as saying stuff to God. Then I met a guy named Juan Carlos Ortiz, and he taught me how to pray. Juan Carlos believes that prayer has much more to do with listening than it does talking. And he's right. Prayer has a lot less to do with worrying and more to do with being in God's presence—listening to him. Juan Carlos told me he would go to a river one day a week, and he'd spend the whole day there. He'd go to this special place and sit down and he'd say, "All right, God, I'm here." Then he'd just sit back against a tree and cross his arms. That's how Juan Carlos prays, and he's a spiritual giant. I started doing that on Fridays eight years ago and it has transformed my inner life.

When you pray, don't worry. Prayer means creating space for you and God. So I'm calling you out. If you want to be a real disciple of Jesus, do more than go to church. Start by taking twenty minutes in the morning to spend with God. And if you're falling asleep in your room, then go to a park or somewhere beautiful with a cup of coffee. Go somewhere you love, somewhere beautiful, and just say, "All right, God, I'm here." And you can start with the Lord's Prayer. Say something like, "Our Father, the one who fills the heavens, we treasure and value your name. We want what you want. Give us what we need. No more, no less. Lead us not into temptation. Help us to live righteous lives. We want your kingdom, your power, and your glory.

When you fast, do not look somber as the hypocrites do, for they disfigure their faces to show others they are fasting. Truly I tell you, they have received their reward in full. But when you fast, put oil on your head and wash your face, so that it will not be obvious to others that you are fasting, but only to your Father, who is unseen; and your Father, who sees what is done in secret, will reward you.

—Matthew 6:16–18

12 Feasting on the Spirit

"FASTING IS FEASTING on the Spirit."

These powerful words shared with me by my mentor Bill changed my view of both fasting and asceticism. Perhaps you never fasted before unless it was some kind of a health thing your sister or chiropractor gave you. Many people do not understand what fasting is for the spiritual life.

Fasting is an important teaching of the Sermon on the Mount. In this chapter we'll take a closer look at this spiritual discipline.

Purpose of Fasting

Jesus says in the Sermon on the Mount, "When you fast, do not look somber as the hypocrites do, for they disfigure their faces to show others they are fasting. Truly I tell you, they have received their reward in full. But when you fast, put oil on your head and wash your face, so that it will not be obvious to others that you are fasting, but only to your Father, who is unseen; *and your Father, who sees what is done in secret, will reward you*" (Matthew 6:16–18).

Let's look closely at that last sentence. What reward is Jesus is talking about?

This verse says we should not do things to prove ourselves spiritually to others. Do you ever find yourself caught in this trap? Whether it's fasting, helping a neighbor, giving to the poor, meeting physical needs of others, praying, worshipping, or going to church—you originally did it simply because it was good. Somewhere along the way, however, you found yourself doing it to receive the affirmation of others.

When we do things to prove something spiritually, even to ourselves, we have totally missed the point of the gospel. Fasting, as well as any other spiritual discipline, cannot be about trying to get people to like and accept you more. It cannot even be about you trying to like and accept yourself more. We must learn what grace is. Grace is the unmerited favor and love of God—the ferocious, undying love God has for you. This love and power does for us what we cannot do on our own.

So fasting is feasting. When we fast we are putting ourselves in a place of devouring spiritual bread, which is Jesus. When we fast, it's not for spiritual kudos. It's not to say, "Look how religious and Christian I am." It's to eat the goodness of God.

The Merit-Based Mind-Set

Fasting is all about God's love. Did you know the God we serve in our theology as Christians is the only God in religious thought who loves sinners? Every other image of God is constructed as a reflection of humanity's anger. As the old saying goes, "God made man in his own image, and we returned the favor."

The typical religious view of God is that he is as vicious, unforgiving, and retributive as we are toward each other. That is not the real God. We secretly think we earn God's affection and favor when we are good. We think, *When I'm good God is close to me and loves me, but when I sin God is far from me and angry.* If that's you, you are giving yourself too much credit. God doesn't love you because of your goodness or stop loving you because you've sinned. That's totally contrary to the Christian gospel of grace. We may think, *I know God loves me now, but when I overcome this big vice in my life, then God will love me even more.* Or maybe, *Then God will favor me or bless me or listen to my prayers more.* There's nothing you can do to earn God's closeness, love, or pleasure. Isn't that great news?

How often do we, as Christians, view our relationship with God as based on our own merit? It's almost impossible for us to understand that a holy and perfect God actually loves us in our sin, our brokenness, our addictions, our hatred, and our anger. Even then, God loves us, adores us, favors us, blesses us, and hears our prayers. That's Christianity because that's grace. It's hard to believe because most of the love we've experienced in life has been based on merit. In our experience, goodness comes with reward and badness comes with consequence. There is not one person in this world who would love you or stay close to you if you were evil enough, so how could God be that way?

The merit-based view of self-worth begins in school with grades. When you were in elementary school and didn't do good work, you got a C or a D, while another student got an A or a B. And as you progressed in school, you started to realize, *If I work hard, my school and my parents accept me in a better way.*

This mind-set starts to weave into everything we do. *If I work hard, press hard, and take hold of opportunity, then great things will happen. But when I am less efficient, less bold, and take fewer risks, then I start to fail. When I mess up, I need to hide my blunders and manage my reputation.*

So we start to think that our relationship with God is based on what we have, what we do, and what people say about us. *If I really pray a lot, God's going to listen more and bless me more. If I give a lot more to charity, if I overcome my vices, and if I attend church regularly, then I'll come a little bit closer to God's love.*

But that mentality gets everything backwards. You cannot become a virtuous, Jesus kind of person by trying harder. It begins and ends with the power that comes from knowing this: *I'm not what I have, not what I do, and not what people say about me. I'm God's child and he loves me. This love cannot increase and it cannot decrease. He loves me just as I am.*

Your life is not a disappointment to God. He sees all the skeletons in your closet. He knows all the hidden things of your heart. He knows the things you haven't told anybody. He knows your past and even knows your future. He loves you and is proud of the fact that you exist because he made you. He knows the deepest parts of you and still loves you.

All the things we talk about in the Sermon on the Mount— the way we treat people, the way we try to not be angry—are a waste of our time if we do not understand God's deep, precious, and ferocious love for us. We are his sons and daughters. He's pleased in us, takes great pleasure in our existence, and treasures each of us.

Do You Believe God Loves You?

Brennan Manning, a great spiritual thinker and author, discovered this in his own life after trying to muscle out a strong spirituality. He said that in the twilight of his life, after spending thousands of hours in solitude and prayer, he came to believe in his heart that when we die and come to face God on Judgment Day, God will ask us one question, and one question alone. He will ask us, when we're standing there before him: "Did you believe that I loved you?"[1]

The true believers will say, "Yes, Lord, I knew you loved me, even in my wretchedness and my sin and my brokenness, in my hurting. Even in my loathing and in my lack of work and laziness and all of those things, I knew you loved me."

Sometimes I wonder, what would I say? When God can see the depths of my heart and words don't matter because he already knows what I did and what I think, can I say, "Yes, I knew truly, my whole life, that you loved me"? Can I say to him, "The knowledge of your love inspired everything I did in faith and religion, and the way I treated my neighbor. Everything came from knowing that you loved me"?

Some of us on that day will admit, "No, Lord, I didn't know you loved me." Nevertheless, I think even for those of us who say that, he will say, "Welcome and know my love now." God's love is so grand and so rich and so unending that if you don't know it now, you will know it then. And you'll wish you had carried it with you through life because all morality, all goodness, all strength comes from deeply understanding and knowing God's love.

Brennan Manning described Judgment Day in *The Ragamuffin Gospel*.

> Because salvation is by grace through faith, I believe that among the countless number of people standing in front of the throne and in front of the Lamb, . . . I shall see the prostitute from the Kit-Kat Ranch in Carson City, Nevada, who tearfully told me that she could find no other employment to support her two-year-old son. I shall see the woman who had an abortion and is haunted by guilt and remorse . . . the deathbed convert who for decades . . . broke every law of God and man. . . .
>
> There they are, there we are—the multitude who so wanted to be faithful, who at times got defeated, soiled by life . . . but through it all, clung to the faith.
>
> My friends, if this is not good news to you, you have never understood the gospel of grace.[2]

All of us are broken. The only perfect person you know is a person you don't know at all. God sees what you could be and he knows what you should be, but he loves you just as you are. And until we get there, nothing else matters. All holiness, all righteous living, all goodness can only naturally come from a place of intimacy and understanding God's unending, perfect, meritless love for his kids.

Our Need for Intimacy

The human soul cries out for intimacy. Every part of our soul cries out for deep connection. We were created this way. Yet we live in a fallen world that is disconnected and fragmented. In our nature is a desire to be reconnected with God and with people. That is why being lonely is such a horrible feeling because you become acutely aware of your separation from people and God. It is against your nature to be this way, so it's painful. And when the soul cries out for intimacy, the body cries out for intimacy. Here's where fasting comes in.

The body cries out for intimacy. And when the body cries out for intimacy, the typical American or Westerner thinks this: *My body is crying out for intimacy, so I will give it food or sex, I will give it media, I will give it some shopping. I will stay busy, I will call a friend, and maybe he or she can meet my need.* When the body cries out for intimacy and we give it food, busyness, shopping, or media, these good things become perverse and harmful. Though in their essence they are blessings from God, they become warped because we are trying to cram them into a place they were not made to fill. They mutate; they become monsters. They feel good, and that's the worst thing. They move from simple distraction to a drug to medicate our deep pain and loneliness.

So good food becomes gluttony. Wine with a friend becomes alcoholism. A beautiful film becomes pornography or unrealistic fantasies of romantic love. Shopping becomes greed and indebtedness. Busyness becomes unbridled restlessness.

As we continue to tailspin, our bodies cry out even more for intimacy. So we say, *Here's more food, here's more media, here's more busyness, more friends, and more stuff, and I'll buy more things!* This cycle is a broken part of human existence. Our bodies cry out for intimacy, and our bodies need to be conquered with God's love.

God Loves Your Body

Did you know God loves your body? Some of you are thinking, *I don't love this body.* Our bodies are super weird in many ways. I won't go into detail how. I remember during the journey from being a child to being a teenager thinking, *Oh, my body does this now. That's cool!* You can run faster, jump higher. Then as you get older you think, *Oh, my body does this now.* A few aches, some stiffness, gray hair. We can't eat certain foods, or we need medications. Our bodies change constantly.

Even though we may hate our bodies, God loves them. Learn this principle: God loves your body.

The body is an important part of old-school Christian theology. To the early Christians this fact was essential: Jesus was resurrected from the dead in his real physical body with holes in his hands and in his feet. That's a non-negotiable orthodox Christian teaching. In the days of the Bible, a group called the Gnostics taught that Jesus was raised only in spirit because, in their view, only the spirit mattered. This heresy is called Docetism. These Gnostics were considered enemies of the Christian church. Because of this there are many written responses by Christian thinkers, documents defending the view of the sacred body. It's not just the spirit that matters, but the body also matters because God loves the body. Amid all of its aging, sickness, brokenness, and white hairs, God chooses to call your body his temple. That matters. If you start to meditate on this, it will change your spirituality in a big way.

Many of the things we experience in life—not just hunger, but things like lust or anger, or even the compulsive need to buy things—are deeply connected with what's happening in our bodies. It's as if, at some level, your mind has been renewed and your spirit has been renewed, but not your body. You have parts of your body that are arguing with your mind. You say in your mind, *I'm not going to eat that chocolate cake*, but your body says, *Yes, you are.* We say, "I'm too fat. I'm too skinny. I'm too tall. I'm too old. I'm too young. I'm too hairy." Regardless of all the ways you don't like your body, God loves your body and wants to train it, subdue it, and conquer it with his love.

You see, when we don't understand God's love, our body cries out for intimacy, for all carnal pleasures. Our body just screams for it. And like scratching a mosquito bite, when you give in to those carnal pleasures, for a minute it feels a little better, but later your body wants it even more. What the body truly wants—what it's screaming out for—is intimacy with God, to truly know God's love.

Training Your Body for God's Love

Many of us think the word *heart* in Scripture refers to the emotions. But in the Bible, the heart does not mean your emotions. Follow your heart, for example, does not mean to follow your emotions. The heart is your will. In classical philosophy and in the Bible, the heart means the very essence of who you are as a person. It means what you choose to do.

In the Bible, the emotions allegorically live in the belly. And that's why the old-school mystics believed in fasting. Fasting was a way in which you could attack the place where your emotions dwell. Often, when I start getting short or on edge with my wife, Hannah, she very calmly looks at me, puts a hand on my shoulder, and says, "I love you."

I say, "I love you too. Why are you saying that?"

She asks, "Have you eaten lately?"

I say, "No, but maybe I will now."

Many of us are that way. When you're hungry, you tend to hurry and be a little on edge. So there's something about fasting, then, that impacts the emotions. It's a way of moving away from a place where we constantly give in to what our bodies want—like eating, shopping, media, busyness, going out, or drinking. It's a way of saying, "I'm going to step back from that physical pleasure and, in the midst of my intentional hunger, simply feast on the good things of God." Fasting is a way of training and subduing your body to come in harmony with the love of God. It's a way of emptying that inner hole to create room for the Spirit.

Fasting is one of the three big disciplines Jesus talks about in the Sermon on the Mount. The first is giving to charity, the second is prayer, and the third is fasting. Fasting, probably more than any spiritual discipline, brings your body into harmony with God's love. It teaches you to think, *I don't need to eat right now. I don't need to give my body what it wants all the time.* That's a good thing because it teaches us to eat or consume media and other things from a healthy place. Then these things can bless your life in a nourishing way.

How to Fast

If you want to fast, this is how you do it:

- Make sure you talk to your doctor before you fast because if you're diabetic or have certain other medical issues, you can't fast from food. You have to give up something else like hurrying or surfing the Internet.
- If you're going to fast, if you've never done it before, consider fasting for just one lunch.
- If you want to fast for an entire day, I suggest you start after dinner so that you fast one dinner to the next and just drink water for a day.
- If you want to fast for three days, this is what I suggest: get a bottle of fresh-squeezed apple juice (the kind that's not clear but looks cloudy), and do one part apple juice, two parts water, so you're drinking a lot of water with a little bit of apple juice in it. The first day is difficult, the second day is torturous, and the third

day is euphoric. On that third day, at least for me, you feel like you've conquered it.

- Whatever you do, don't fast to prove anything to yourself. Don't do it to prove anything to anybody else. Do it to subdue your body, train it, and teach it that it is loved by God and it doesn't need food. And it also teaches you about other things too. There may be other things instead of food from which you may need to fast.

The main point of this is simply to understand that our bodies are in a state of brokenness and are out of alignment with the Spirit of God, who says, "I love you. I love you not as you can be or will be someday, or as you should be—I love you just as you are right now."

How many of us on Judgment Day will be able to stand before God and say, "Yes, Lord, I believed truly with all my heart that you loved me"? Many of us won't be able to say that. And God will say, "Oh, how I wish you knew."

You are not a disappointment to God. You are loved and cherished, needed, and wanted, not because of what you do, not because of what you have, and not because of what anybody says about you. You are loved and valued because of who you are.

Do not store up for yourselves treasures on earth, where moths and vermin destroy, and where thieves break in and steal. But store up for yourselves treasures in heaven, where moths and vermin do not destroy, and where thieves do not break in and steal. For where your treasure is, there your heart will be also.

The eye is the lamp of the body. If your eyes are healthy, your whole body will be full of light. But if your eyes are unhealthy, your whole body will be full of darkness. If then the light within you is darkness, how great is that darkness!

No one can serve two masters. Either you will hate the one and love the other, or you will be devoted to the one and despise the other. You cannot serve both God and money.

—Matthew 6:19–24

13 Spiritual Wealth

I WANT TO CHALLENGE the Western myth that says money makes us safe and free. The main reason people want money today is for safety and freedom. For many, money means better doctors, moving to a safer neighborhood, and putting food on the table. We think, *When I have more money, I can go where I want. I can work less. Money can give these things to me.* Some of the richest people on earth think if they just have a little more, they will be safe and free.

But you don't need money to be safe and free. You can be safe and free now, regardless of how much money you make. You are safe and free right now if you're in the shepherding of Jesus. That's the only thing that matters. That's one of the most important lessons we learn: if you know Christ, there is no loss that cannot be redeemed. So how does that affect our view of money?

Is Money Good or Bad?

Is money a good thing or a bad thing? It's like asking if fire is a good thing or a bad thing. It depends on who has it.

Money is something we want our kids to understand and respect. It was really important to my dad that I understand money. He would take, for example, ten oranges and line them up. "Okay, Bobby," he'd say, "here are ten oranges. This is your harvest from your tree. What do you do with those ten oranges? One orange goes to the church, two oranges go to the bank, and seven oranges you get to eat." That's what you do with money, and that's what I was trained to do growing up. Anytime I get ten dollars, one dollar goes to the church, two dollars goes to the savings account, and seven dollars I spend on bills or whatever. I learned other valuable money tips from my parents like don't go into debt and don't buy things you can't afford. That is what we grew up learning. And really, as far as managing money goes, if you understand that, you've got about 90 percent of it down. Of course, that's a hard thing to do in a world that focuses on material gain, bases prestige on what kind of car you drive, and stereotypes you based on what kind of house you have. Money is important to just about everyone.

Now, when I was a kid, I was unique in that I actually liked money. I didn't just like the things money could buy; I liked money itself. I collected it. In fact, I have this little treasure chest. It's ornate, with pearls on top, and it fits nicely on a bookshelf. As a kid I always kept it close. Inside, I had a Buffalo nickel that I thought would be worth millions of dollars someday. I had a gold nugget I found at a real gold mine in Arizona. I had a rock in the shape of a sock that I found on Catalina Island. I also had a small collection of old pennies, a pearl I pulled from an oyster, and a picture of my parents when they were still married. I had all of these treasures safely tucked away in my little chest on the shelf.

So when I read the Sermon on the Mount and thought about "treasures in heaven," I pictured treasures to be physical things in heaven like gold and crowns with jewels. I imagined it like this: *I'll help an old lady cross the street and get a silver coin in heaven. And someday when I die, the size of my heavenly house will be based on all the good things I did in this life. And if I'm really good, my house will have a treasure room. So I'm going to live such a good life that my house in heaven is going to have its own treasure trove. I will earn different crowns, and they'll be like trophies. People will marvel.*

As an older child, I continued to carry this childish view of heavenly rewards. Then when I became an adult, the idea of heavenly treasure became something that was almost disgusting to me, something I still believed but was no longer interested in at all. I still sort of thought it to be the truth, just not a truth that appealed to me. (If the streets are paved with gold, wouldn't my treasure room just be holding a bunch of pavement?)

I'm happy to tell you this view of treasure in heaven is not what Jesus is trying to communicate to us. Treasures in heaven are not physical wealth in a metaphysical afterlife. If that's what you think, then it's no wonder you have no desire to store up for yourselves treasures in heaven. Receiving jewels and gold someday far off is not what Jesus is talking about when he talks about treasures in heaven. It's not money you receive at some later time in your spiritual existence. In fact, treasures in heaven are something you access right now. They are available to you as a believer right now.

The Kingdom of Heaven

The kingdom of heaven was the main thesis of Jesus' ministry. It's interchangeable with another phrase, *the kingdom of God*. Jesus is talking about these two phrases all the time. They basically mean the reign of God through Jesus the King. It means that what God wants done in this world, God gets done. It's linked to that part of the Lord's Prayer where Jesus says, "Your kingdom come, your will be done, on earth as it is in heaven" (Matthew 6:10). It's the idea that he wants earth ruled by God's kingdom.

When Jesus talks about the kingdom of heaven, the original Greek says "the heavens," and that's important. In a first-century Jewish worldview, "the heavens" didn't just mean heaven, where we go to be with the Lord when we die. It also meant the stars, the sky, and the physical space around us. The kingdom of the heavens is not just something far away. It is something present, nearby, like the air. You walk in it and breathe it in. It's "at hand" or "in your hands" or "in your midst," as Jesus would say (Luke 17:21).

When Jesus is talking about the kingdom of the heavens, he's talking about the kingdom that's in the air around you that comes from a place called heaven. It's not much different than the way we talk about a modern nation state. America is a place, but it's also a government, and a culture, and songs, and food, and people. It's not just sea to shining sea either because when you walk into an American embassy in Germany, you are technically standing on American soil. You are under the authority of America. Likewise the kingdom of heaven is a real place, but it's also present wherever its citizens are: in their bodies, their words, the way they eat, the songs they sing, and the manner in which they pledge their allegiance. When Jesus announces the kingdom of the heavens, he is saying it is here right now—all around us.

Treasures in Heaven

So when Jesus talks about storing up treasures in heaven, he's talking about storing up something of value in this spiritual air around us and in heaven when we die. It's both. This is the thing that is lost to most of us: there are treasures we can store up for ourselves, spiritual treasures we can access right now that cannot be diminished or taken away. They are available to us right now. Spiritual wealth can't be changed or taken away. Almost everyone has spiritual treasures, though they may not realize it.

Something similar to spiritual wealth would be one's education. If you studied and received your engineering degree, it would cost you a lot of money. Although there are many ways people could take your money, no one could take away your engineering education. They could take your diploma, but they could never take away your knowledge of how to build an axle. You would always have that. There is something intangible and untarnishable about knowledge. Spiritual treasures are like an education, but even better. They don't fade or wither, and they cannot be taken from their possessor. They endure for eternity.

All of us treasure something. Jesus says, "Where your treasure is, there your heart will be also" (Matthew 6:21). Everyone has treasures. Treasure is a most human thing. My kids have their treasures. My daughter's treasure is her brown blanket. She has two blankets: one is pink and one is brown, but for whatever reason, the brown one is the one she treasures. She needs it when she sleeps or else she flips out. Since my son was a toddler, he has had a little plastic turkey. It's about the size of a tennis ball, and he always has it. If he drops it as you take him out of his car seat, he goes, "Uh-oh, uh-oh, uh-oh!" He lets us know that he needs that turkey.

What Do You Treasure?

Many of us have things we treasure and value in our lives—trinkets and knickknacks. I've worked with homeless people for years, and it's amazing the things they treasure. I had a friend, Jay, who used to come to church every Sunday. He always came to church with two big black trash bags filled with his treasures. I'd let him put the plastic bags in my office so they would be safe. These two gigantic plastic bags were filled with his "documents." He treasured those. They were with him all the time.

What do you treasure? What do you value even though others may not understand? Jesus says we should treasure spiritual things because if we treasure spiritual things, those things can't be tarnished, they can't be taken away from us, and even when we die, they'll be available to us. We should treasure spiritual things.

To understand this concept of treasures in heaven, imagine Bear Grylls (the famous retired commando survivalist) and an investment banker. These two people treasure different things. The investment banker treasures money, securities, stocks, and bonds. Bear Grylls values flint, backpacks, knives, and fire. Bear Grylls is the ultimate survivalist. He's the British version of a Navy SEAL, retired. He's on this crazy show where he goes around surviving in the worst conditions with nothing, builds lean-tos, and eats the most disgusting stuff.

Imagine you were to drop off this investment banker and Bear Grylls in New York. Who is going to do better on Wall Street? The investment banker is, of course. He's going to know all the best restaurants, he's going to know what to invest in, and he's probably going to be up to date on all the latest shows. But if you drop those same two men in the middle of the Sahara or a forest in Siberia, that investment banker will be useless. With all of his money and all the things he has, he has no treasure in that dangerous place. Bear Grylls is the man for that environment. Because of the things Grylls treasures, he will thrive, and the investment banker will look to him for help like a beggar.

We live in a spiritual environment that requires spiritual resources to live a spiritual life with real power. If we treasure spiritual things rather than material things we will grow with the kind of knowledge that will help us thrive in the jungle that is life.

The Problem of Wealth

Moths and rust do destroy it all. You can have all the money in the world, and all it takes is one health disaster and all that money could be wiped away. You can have tons and tons of money and one lawsuit takes it all. Or there could be one change in government policy and your property or business is gone.

Sometimes I feel really bad for my wealthy friends because everybody thinks they don't have the same problems as everyone else, but they do! They still suffer. The only difference is that nobody feels bad for them. There's no sympathy. And the funny thing is, if you are reading this in the industrialized world you are likely living like a king compared to those living in the other two-thirds of the world. They think you have no problems because of all your treasures.

So if you're wealthy and you have assets, you have to hedge against lawsuits, theft, and people pretending to be your friends to get your stuff. You are continually inundated with requests. Your money and your assets are constantly being threatened. It is simply not true that if someone has more money and more assets, he or she will be freer and safer.

Money is a good thing, but don't put your trust in money. Most wealthy people can tell you money is great but it's not going to keep you safe. It's not going to protect you. It's certainly not going to make you freer in the long run.

Where Are You Looking?

Jesus goes on to say in this passage, "The eye is the lamp of the body. If your eyes are healthy, your whole body will be full of light. But if your eyes are unhealthy, your whole body will be full of darkness. If then the light within you is darkness, how great is that darkness!" (Matthew 6:22–23).

Jesus describes the eyes as the portals through which things enter your body and soul. He's asking his audience to imagine that their eyes are like two little windows and the body is a dark room. All the light that shines into your body this way comes through your eyes.

In other words, what you look at will illuminate your mind, your heart, and your body. If you spend your time looking for only material things, that light will be darkness. But if you spend your life looking for spiritual things and the kingdom of God, your whole body and your whole life will be illuminated with God's goodness.

Of course, it's hard not to think in terms of money. Every single day you make important economic decisions. You wake up, you need some gas, so you find the right gas station with a good price. You fill up, and then maybe you go to Starbucks. You decide to get regular coffee instead of a latte to save some money. You have to pay bills. You give money to charities. You buy lunch, you buy something for your friend for their birthday, you buy some paper towels, and you send off a check for the electric bill. Every day, you're probably making five or six important economic decisions and about a hundred more unimportant ones.

How many times do you want to do something but you can't because you don't have the money? It's how I feel many times when I'm sitting on a plane traveling somewhere. I look at those people in business class. I'm six foot three, so when I sit in these tiny little planes my knees hit the seat in front of me. I see those people in first class and think, *That would be so nice.* But the guy in first class is thinking, *Man, I had to wait in line, check in my baggage. I want a private jet.* There's always something better. We always compare up, not down.

The Thorny Thing about Money

Jesus calls the pleasures of money and wealth and riches of this life the thorns that choke out the word of God that was planted in your heart (Mark 4:18–19). God puts a seed, or a word, in your heart and it begins to grow and flourish. Then it quickly comes under attack. The first attack is the troubles of this life. Jesus tells us we must be rooted and grounded if we are to get through this first attack. Many of us really shine when going through troubles and actually grow deeper in our relationship with God and others. We see that seed in our heart continue to grow.

However, if God's Word takes root and starts to grow, the second thing to attack it is money and pleasure. If the troubles don't break us, then comforts will. How many of us have had our dreams die on a vine because our decisions were based purely on money and safety? We abandon that great nonprofit business idea and flee to the haven of complacency or comfort. We abandon God's call to invest in our children, mentor, or volunteer because we have to put in more hours at work. We abandon God's dream or call to us so we can have the safety of a good paycheck. Too many of us are more afraid of losing our house than we are of losing our dreams.

The truth is, if you get really good at something, if you pursue your vision from God and do something that you love, then you're probably going to make a lot more money than you would have doing some job that you hate. Don't wait until you have enough money saved up to do what you are called to do. We tend to think, *When I have enough money, I'll be independent. When I have enough money someday, then I'll be able to do what I was born to do.* Do what you want to do now. Live in the reality of God's kingdom right now. Follow Jesus today.

Be generous with your time and money. I've seen many people who couldn't get their idea off the ground. They couldn't find a way to succeed. They had these dreams, but they couldn't fulfill them. But when they decided just to start helping people, success came.

My friend Jeff had a business that wasn't going anywhere; he was struggling. Then he fell in love with ministering to teenagers. So he decided to help with after-school programs. In a few years of putting all his extra money into buying video games and teaching the Bible to these teenagers, creating community for them, all of a sudden his business exploded and he made more money than ever. I think this is because he stopped looking for money and started looking for his calling. He started looking for God's action and life in young people around him. He started living for something more important than money. From that point on, money was no longer an end in itself but a means to fulfill God's purpose in his life, to help those in need.

Your Spiritual Portfolio

God wants you to have a spiritual portfolio. He wants you to be spiritually rich and spiritually wealthy in treasure that cannot be taken away from you. What does your spiritual portfolio look like today? What are the spiritual treasures that you value? What have you built up within the heavens that is blessing your life?

Heavenly treasures look like God's favor. Heavenly treasures look like wisdom. They look like virtue, prudence, justice, love, and mercy. Spiritual treasures look like true happiness. That deep chasm is filled, and you're living with joy and meaning.

Your spiritual wealth is found in your calling, and that calling is more than saving 10 percent for retirement. God has called you to something huge and it's much more than money. If you pursue that thing, you'll have all the money you need. Never let money choke out the word of God that is planted in your heart.

You have a call, you have a mission, and only you can figure it out. And if you're going to succeed in that, you need spiritual treasures. You need to learn how to store up these treasures and access them at key points in your life. God loves you and wants to bless you, but not to the point that it harms your soul.

Therefore I tell you, do not worry about your life, what you will eat or drink; or about your body, what you will wear. Is not life more than food, and the body more than clothes? Look at the birds of the air; they do not sow or reap or store away in barns, and yet your heavenly Father feeds them. Are you not much more valuable than they? Can any one of you by worrying add a single hour to your life?

And why do you worry about clothes? See how the flowers of the field grow. They do not labor or spin. Yet I tell you that not even Solomon in all his splendor was dressed like one of these. If that is how God clothes the grass of the field, which is here today and tomorrow is thrown into the fire, will he not much more clothe you—you of little faith? So do not worry, saying, "What shall we eat?" or "What shall we drink?" or "What shall we wear?" For the pagans run after all these things, and your heavenly Father knows that you need them. But seek first his kingdom and his righteousness, and all these things will be given to you as well. Therefore do not worry about tomorrow, for tomorrow will worry about itself. Each day has enough trouble of its own.

—Matthew 6:25–34

14 Birds and Lilies

YOU DON'T HAVE TO WORRY.

This is a large part of the good news of the kingdom of God, but it stands in stark contrast to a world that would have us think otherwise. In the Sermon on the Mount, we learn that God is in control and that when we live in the shepherding of Jesus, we really have nothing to worry about.

Jesus tells us, "Seek first [God's] kingdom and his righteousness, and all these things will be given to you as well. Therefore, do not worry about tomorrow, for tomorrow will worry about itself. Each day has enough trouble of its own" (Matthew 6:33–34).

These words were spoken to an audience of people who had much to worry about. Many of them were sick and poor. Probably many of the people who were listening to Jesus really weren't interested in what he had to say. They were there because they wanted to see the new celebrity, the new famous rabbi. Some of them were there because they heard he could heal people. They may have been thinking, *If I listen to the message, then I might get my time with him and get something out of it.*

Jesus is preaching about what really matters. In fact, the reason he's healing people is not just because he wants them to be well, but he wants them to see that he's living in a different reality. So he begins teaching. He tells all of them, "Do not worry about your life, what you will eat or drink; or about your body, what you will wear. Is not life more than food, and the body more than clothes?" (Matthew 6:25). Imagine he's standing there and, as he's talking, there are hurting people, sick people, elderly people, people who have lost everything. Jesus says to them, "Don't worry."

As he's standing there talking, I imagine that a warm wind blows off the Sea of Galilee. Jesus looks up and he sees some birds at play. How easygoing and lofty their lives are. He says, "Look at the birds of the air; they do not sow or reap or store away in barns" (v. 26). They don't have a 401k, a Roth IRA, or a pension. Jesus continues, "Yet your heavenly Father feeds them. Are you not much more valuable than they?"

Then Jesus says, "Can any one of you by worrying add a single hour to your life?" (v. 27). Imagine that warm wind is still blowing, and maybe it blows through the wildflowers growing on the hill. These are flowers that nobody planted and yet they're beautiful—lilacs, lilies, and daisies. And they bend and sway in the wind.

He says:

> And why do you worry about clothes? See
> how the flowers of the field grow. They do
> not labor or spin. Yet I tell you that not even
> Solomon in all his splendor was dressed like
> one of these. If that is how God clothes the
> grass of the field, which is here today and to-
> morrow is thrown into the fire, will he not
> much more clothe you—you of little faith?
> So do not worry, saying, 'What shall we eat?'
> or 'What shall we drink?' or 'What shall we
> wear?' For the pagans run after all these
> things, and your heavenly Father knows that
> you need them. But seek first his kingdom and
> his righteousness, and all these things will be
> given to you as well. Therefore do not worry
> about tomorrow, for tomorrow will worry
> about itself. Each day has enough trouble of
> its own. (vv. 28–34)

The message Jesus is giving us is this: don't worry, relax,
seek the kingdom, and it will be all right. This message is
very different than the modern message we hear from most
people today.

Our Worried World

Think about the people Jesus is talking to and the violence and volatility of their world. They're occupied by a foreign power, the Romans. The average life span is in the forties. It's very dangerous to have a baby. It's easy to get a cold or infection that can threaten your life or disable you. Food is not plentiful. There are no social programs. You never know what kinds of things people are plotting against you or your tribe. It's a dangerous world. And Jesus tells them not to worry.

When you think of standards of living, if you compare this world to that one, who has more to worry about? Clearly they do. If we had to deal with the things the people in the ancient world had to deal with, we would just fall apart. Look at that world and how difficult it was, and Jesus says they don't have to worry about anything? God is going to take care of them?

To push this point even further, never has any society in human history had better living conditions, better health, better medicine, or been more safe than American citizens today. Yet studies show there has never been a society more anxious and worried than today's America. What does that say about material possessions, filled silos, and big bank accounts, or safety in general and its ability to make us feel relaxed and happy? It says plainly that worry, anxiety, and happiness are likely unrelated to affluence. In all likelihood, affluent places like America may be worried in proportion to their financial success. Doesn't it just seem odd that America is the wealthiest, safest, and still most worried country in the world?

We live in a culture that is training us to worry. Furthermore, the people who are training us to worry benefit the more we worry. Every morning I get up and turn on the news. I listen to the news on the radio in my car. I hear about all the kids who are being abducted, the people who are being raped, and all the violence that's going on in the world. And during a pleasant drive through the hills, I hear about fires, earthquakes, and looming threats. As I grow worried about these things I feel obliged to hear more so I'm not left in the dark. As I gather more information I feel even more worried and even more dependent on the news. Then I hear their commercials. Because I hear their commercials they make money. All the while I don't even notice the beauty of the world I'm driving through. So the news agency benefits by having bad news. Bad news is good news for the Associated Press. This is why the news media is training us to be worried. The more we worry, the more attention they get and the more money they make.

I did my undergraduate degree in marketing. At the time we were learning that the old mantra of "find a need and fill it" had been replaced with a new axiom: "create a need and fill it." After all, why find a need when you can just make one? This, of course, is the driving force behind modern business. The goal is to convince you of the need for a new cell phone for purposes of social standing, efficiency, happiness, and so on. You don't simply want it; you need it. Oh yeah, and they are happy to help you fill that need.

This rampant consumerism in our culture is only made worse by our incredible expectations. As we watch reality television, read pop-culture magazines, or see advertisements, our anticipation for what we hope to be or own gets terribly out of sync with God's kingdom. The world frames what our house ought to look like, what our friends ought to be like, or how our spouse ought to treat us. And as those unmet expectations remain unfulfilled, we worry.

I feel particularly bad for young women today because of the way magazines and movies portray beauty. They pick the most gorgeous woman they can find, put her in an expensive outfit with professional makeup and the best lighting possible, and that is still not pretty enough. So they use a computer to make her waist smaller, her breasts bigger, her hair longer, and her face younger. Now there is this fake image that everybody sees. Then many young women look in the mirror and compare. Often this results in worry and all of its consequences like eating disorders, debt, and a slew of personal mistakes related to low self-worth.

We live with so many unrealistic expectations. We worry about settling for the wrong person. We worry about our reputation, about how we look, and about what people think about us. We worry about our kids. We worry about our politics, the national debt, the environment, and everything. Our lives are poisoned by worry. We can't just enjoy today.

To this Jesus says something like, "Stop worrying. Smile. Today's a gift. Relax. You're going to be okay. I'm in control." With all the changes that happen in a scary world, a good, powerful, and loving God is in control. That is good news.

The Day to Stop Worrying

Many of us live in a constant state of worry. Do you know the biblical word for worry has its roots in "choking" or "being strangled"? That's what it feels like, doesn't it? The apostle Paul says we are running in a spiritual race (1 Corinthians 9:24–25). Yet for many of us, that sense of worry is like trying to run a marathon while you have asthma. You try to do good work. You're trying to persevere and do the right thing, to help people and live a good Christian life, but you are still worried about so much.

For many of us, there is this one future date that lives in our imagination. It's a little ambiguous, but we know that someday something will happen where all the stars will align and we're not going to have to worry anymore. I remember, when I was in high school, I thought that "someday" was when I would go to college. I thought, *When I graduate high school and I don't have to live in this room, I'm going to go to college where I can just take the classes I want.* When I arrived at college I realized I had to write ten-page papers. I had deadlines. College was expensive and it was hard to find work because I needed time to study. I wanted to meet a girl but couldn't afford one. Now I had a whole new list of challenges. I began to think, *I have no money right now but when I'm done with college, I'll get a job and I'll have money.* I graduated, I got my job, and I started thinking, *Someday when I retire . . .* And this is how life goes. There's always some future date, a date when we think we will be completely safe and will have no need to worry.

183

Unless that day is today, it will never come. A few years ago, a story called "An Interview with God" began circulating anonymously on the Internet; it gained such popularity that it was ultimately published in book form. As the story goes, God agrees to an interview on the subject of mankind. The things God finds surprising about mankind include losing their health to make money, then losing the money to restore their health; worrying so anxiously about the future that they forget the present; and living as though they will never die, only to die without having really lived.[1]

Today is the best day to stop worrying. If you're looking for something to worry about, trust me, you will find it. Stop looking for things to worry about and start living.

Seeing What Is Really There

I know what many are thinking. If you're the realist, you want to shake me and say, "Bobby, I'm trying to be responsible! Nobody is responsible. I'm always the one who has to be responsible for everything and everyone." I have a feeling you couldn't be irresponsible even if you tried. Being responsible and realistic doesn't mean you have to worry. Do the next right thing without worrying. Nobody needs you to be anxious. You can be organized and never worry a day in your life. Isn't that good news? There's nothing you can do worried that you can't do better with peace of mind. Don't imagine all the things that could go wrong. Instead, Jesus teaches us to seek first his kingdom and his righteousness, and all that other stuff is going to be taken care of. That is good news and a promise we can stand on.

We live in a material world that follows spiritual rules, like a stereograph. Stereographs came out in the 1990s. Stereographs are those digitally printed sort of blurry pictures with colorful squares and lines. Within that image is a second hidden image—a three-dimensional picture unrecognizable to those that don't know how to look for it. When stereographs first came out, some could see the hidden 3-D image while others couldn't. Those who couldn't might try for hours or days and never see. Some suggested this was some sort of elaborate trick, concerned that they were being made to appear foolish. Some would pretend to see even though they could not. It took me weeks before I could see.

The stereograph reveals itself to you as though dreaming. At first you can make out only a part of the whole—all of a sudden with some dimension. The key is to look through the image, not at the image. If you look at the image, you can't see it. You have to look past it like it's not there, and as you look through the two-dimensional image, the three-dimensional image starts to take shape.

The one I have on my desk is an image of Jesus on the cross, but you don't know what it is at first. You think, *What is that*? And eventually you see the cross. Then, as you look at it longer, it starts to take on even more shape. Then a soldier with a spear appears. You think, *Wow, I didn't even see that.* You keep staring longer, and then all of a sudden, you see the other two crosses and the hill. You see the whole picture, revealed to you all at once. That is very much what the kingdom of God is like. It remains hidden to those who cannot see through the material world.

Many of us may look right at the image, and we have no idea what's actually there. A disciple is like someone who is able to see through the image and see that there is something three-dimensional there, something that has real value and meaning, something beautiful. But it takes a different kind of looking, and when you can see the world in that way, you realize something very powerful lies under the surface of everything. That "something" is governed by Jesus, and if you are his friend, you don't have to worry about a thing.

I remember when I was in college, there was this kid, Denny, and he was brilliant. He seemed to know everything and excelled in the sciences. There's another optical illusion. I don't know if you've ever seen it, but you see either a vase or two faces. It's both images and you can look at one or the other depending on what you focus on. Denny couldn't see the vase. He could only see the two faces. And what was bizarre is he was probably the smartest guy I had ever met. He was an engineering student, he could solve incredible problems, his IQ was off the charts, and he was superbly intelligent; but when he looked at this very simple image, he couldn't see the vase. All he could see was the two faces looking at each other, and it really bothered him. That's what the spiritual world is like. Some people, in all their brilliance, can't see the simplest thing.

It's like Jesus, who, filled with joy in the Holy Spirit, says, "I praise you, Father, Lord of heaven and earth, because you have hidden these things from the wise and learned, and revealed them to little children. Yes, Father, for this is what you were pleased to do" (Matthew 11:25–26). The kingdom of

God is a spiritual reality underneath the material world, and it's a world that is ruled and governed by God. So, the way we live this life, the kind where we don't worry anymore, is seeking the spiritual world by walking in step and discipleship with Jesus, by seeking what God wants in life and the world, and by releasing our cares to him.

Letting Go of Worry

Worry comes from a place of pride and a need to control. We all need to let go of our pride and trust the Lord.

You don't have to worry about tomorrow, you don't have to worry about all your problems, and you don't have to worry about your kids, your parents, or your spouse. You don't have to worry about the government, you don't have to worry about the environment, and you don't have to worry about money. You don't have to worry about all the things that are actually really important. You can stop worrying right now because God's in control. And yes, be responsible, do the right thing, be a good citizen, be a patron, be a good person, but stop worrying. Stop worrying because there is a spiritual reality in which God is in control. You can smile. You can enjoy the weather today if it is good. You can enjoy your friends and you can stop worrying.

You don't have to be the nag. When you're the worrier, all your friends want you to stop worrying, trust me. They don't need you to be responsible anymore. You can release that too. Everybody is alive for a reason, but many people will miss that reason because they are worried. Don't let that happen to you!

Do not judge, or you too will be judged. For in the same way you judge others, you will be judged, and with the measure you use, it will be measured to you.

Why do you look at the speck of sawdust in your brother's eye and pay no attention to the plank in your own eye? How can you say to your brother, "Let me take the speck out of your eye," when all the time there is a plank in your own eye? You hypocrite, first take the plank out of your own eye, and then you will see clearly to remove the speck from your brother's eye.

Do not give dogs what is sacred; do not throw your pearls to pigs. If you do, they may trample them under their feet, and turn and tear you to pieces.

—Matthew 7:1–6

15 Letting Go of Self-Righteousness

JUDGING OTHERS HAS NO PLACE in the life of a Christian. I encourage Christians to stand for the truth, to stand for what is good, and to stand for what is beautiful and right. But in our standing, we don't push, presume, pretend, judge, worry, and control—instead, we are people who live out that life so that it is so compelling and contagious and desirable that judgment is not needed. We can be encouraging, nice, loving people who see the best in sinners because God saw the best in us when we were sinners.

I remember my first argument with my wife, Hannah. She was my girlfriend at the time. I started criticizing someone I didn't particularly like, someone we both knew. We were in the car, and of course I didn't say my grievances to his face; I said them behind his back. I started telling Hannah all of the things that bothered me about this particular person, one thing after another to the point of getting myself riled up. I went farther and farther with my rant and I turned and I saw her face down. She was crying. She said, "I've never seen you like this. Why do you say things like that about people?"

My wife is someone who always assumes the best about people. She typically believes that if she thinks something bad about someone, she's probably wrong and she's going to find out why. That's one thing that makes me love her so much. Her mantra is, "Always assume the best about people."

I felt like a total jerk. She said, "You can't act that way." And she was right.

As we discuss judging others it is good to know where I am coming from as a pastor. I am talking to you as a former super-legalistic, arrogant, conceited, and self-righteous Pharisee who found Jesus amid his own wretchedness, brokenness, and sinfulness. I found a God who loved me, not as I ought to be, but just as I am, and that changed everything.

The Difference between Judging and Assessing

As believers, we live in a world that has blurred the lines between beautiful and ugly, good and evil, true and false. So there is a part of us that wants to stand up for what is right, what is beautiful, and what is good. From this deep desire for real truth, real goodness, and real beauty, we easily find ourselves in the posture of fighting rather than debating.

Too often that puts us in the position, ironically, where we are doing precisely what is ugly, false, and evil—judging others with an air of self-importance, self-righteousness, and superiority. That's not at all what God has for us as disciples of Jesus.

There's a difference between judging and assessing. This distinction has been taught by many greats from the past. I'll do my best to give you my version. Assessing truth, goodness, and beauty is good. But judging another person is not at all something we get to do as believers. God is the judge. We are his workers. When Jesus talks about judging in the Sermon on the Mount, the kind of judging he is denouncing is when you look at someone's faults and you judge their very essence, who they are. You look at this person and proclaim that they are "less than." They're less than your political party, less than your religious views, less than your patriotism, less than your standards for what is right. They are "less than," not good enough, and outside. They have been judged.

Let me ask you a question: The last time you felt judged, the last time someone confronted you from their high horse, did it help? They came up to you and said, "You know what, you drive way too fast." Let me guess how you responded. You said, "Yes, you're right. I drive way too fast. I'm going to slow down." No, of course that didn't help.

Sometimes someone will confront and judge and it actually helps, but this is very rare and requires the hearer to be incredibly wise and mature. Instead, we ought to begin by assessing. Assessing is not going to someone and saying, "You have a drinking problem." Instead, you say, "You know what, I think you might have a drinking problem, but I love you no matter what. No matter where you go, we're going to get through this together." Do you hear the difference? It's not saying you are "less than"; it's acknowledging, "We're both hurting, we're both broken, and we both have problems. I think you need help, I'm your friend, I love you, and I will do whatever I can to help you get through this." That is solidarity.

Unless you're willing to walk side by side with people in their struggle, their turmoil, their brokenness, or their sin, you have no right to comment on their spiritual walk. If you are not willing to be the one who gets the phone call, who goes there early in the morning, who is there when they cry, who writes them encouraging e-mails, who consistently—not for a little bit, but for weeks, months, or even years—walks with them to help them overcome their difficulties, you have no right to judge where they are spiritually. In other words, if you are going to comment on the morality of someone you care about, then you also have to care enough to be there for them by walking with them through the process of recovery.

Judging the Judgmental People

I realize the irony of sounding very judgmental about judgmental people but that's what Jesus does. Jesus doesn't seem to cast judgment except on one particular group of people, the Pharisees. These men felt it their place to be the judges of all.

In Matthew 7 Jesus says, "Do not judge, or you too will be judged. For in the same way you judge others, you will be judged, and with the measure you use, it will be measured to you" (vv. 1–2).

When we read this scripture, often we think Jesus is saying, "Do not judge others or God is going to judge you from heaven." But that is not what Jesus says. Rather, he says, do not judge or you will "be judged." Perhaps this is rabbinic wisdom about life in general, like the book of Proverbs. Think about this: the people who judge are also the ones who get judged by their neighbors. They don't have a lot of wiggle room to make mistakes. People do not grant them a lot of grace if they mess up.

Jesus is inviting us into a new kind of life where we don't necessarily have to judge others and we don't have to worry about others judging us. He's saying something like, "Do not judge others unless you are willing to live in that arrangement where people also get to judge all of your faults, all of your mistakes, and have commentary on your life, even though they're not going to be involved. They get to do drive-by judging on you, just as you do to others. Don't dish it out if you can't take it."

There is something about being a real-life critic that causes you to be stuck. In the creative world, you have critics—critics who write reviews, critics who make commentary—who have severed themselves from the ability to participate artistically and creatively in the world they critique. Why? Because they've been so critical of others in their field, they know that they cannot go into that world unless they are perfect. All judges and critics are stuck.

Think of Simon Cowell. He is perhaps the world's most famous critic. He is well known for his funny but abrasive criticisms of the singers who do not perform up to snuff. He told one singer her singing was "like cats being squashed." He said to another, "If the criteria was to vote people through for singing every note out of tune, you'd win."[1] But here's the thing . . . although he's jokingly sung at charity events and even on his show, you'll never see a video of Simon Cowell singing in earnest and you never will. Why? Because people would tear him to shreds for anything short of perfection. Simon Cowell will never sing. All judges and critics are stuck in a cage of their own making. That's not what God wants for you. He wants you to be free.

Focus on Your Own Plank

Jesus continues his teaching about judging with a joke. He says, "Why do you look at the speck of sawdust in your brother's eye and pay no attention to the plank in your own eye?" (Matthew 7:3). Everyone would have erupted in laughter. This was a joke of a Jewish kind. Jesus was mocking the hypocrites. You get this picture of a guy, let's call him Eli, with a monstrous piece of wood jutting out of his face, and he walks up to a friend and says, "Hey listen, Joe, we've all been talking and you've got a little something in your eye. You know, there's a speck there. I've got these tweezers, and I think I can help you."

Jesus paints a picture of a hypocrite, a man or woman with a tremendous amount of big personal issues going around trying to fix everyone else. We all know the man or woman who does this. Of course when we are the ones who act this way we are all but blind to our own hypocrisy. Here's the problem with every lesson I give: As I'm talking or writing about judging others, people are thinking about their mom, brother, colleague, or friend who has this vice. People are never thinking of themselves. Most are thinking about someone they know who is judgmental but not evaluating their own judgmental posture. I often do the same thing. That's exactly what this passage is talking about. Don't judge others. Focus on the plank in your own eye.

As a pastor I've found the more vulnerable and honest and real I am, especially about my own struggles, the more power I have to help remove the speck from my brother's eye. I'm not saying, "I'm better than you." I'm saying, "We are in solidarity in this struggle together."

I used to think I was a great chess player. Then I went to a chess club and found out I was a terrible chess player. I used to call myself a theologian, and then I went to seminary. Now when people ask me about theological things, sometimes I say, "I don't know. I used to know, but I don't anymore." There's something about getting good at something that helps you realize you used to be bad at it, and now you're just somewhat okay.

That's what the spiritual life is like. So, as you grow as a moral person, you become more aware of your immorality, darkness, selfishness, and even stupidity, and that's a good thing because it's that very thing that allows you to walk in solidarity with other people. We all need the help of a friend rather than the contempt of a judge. There is solidarity in brokenness. There's even solidarity in sin. When we find that we are sinners, we are broken, and we need help—and when we admit to others we have problems and are broken too—that gives us so much more credibility to help others get on the right path.

Don't Throw Pearls to Pigs

Jesus continues, "Do not give dogs what is sacred; do not throw your pearls to pigs. If you do, they may trample them under their feet, and turn and tear you to pieces" (Matthew 7:6).

Do you put the *mother* in smother? Do you control others "for their own good"? Do you try to shove your ideas down the throats of others to "help them"? That's what this is a bit about. Pigs do not appreciate the value of pearls. A pearl is something of tremendous value. And when you throw something to a pig, they are not looking for something valuable. They're looking for something to eat. If you throw a handful of pearls to a bunch of pigs, they're going to choke.

How many of you have ever said, "I was just trying to help them. Why did they get so mad at me?" Perhaps you gave some advice and the person responded with rage. Maybe you even gave a gift—I mean, a gift! It was a really expensive, nice thing that you know the person wanted, and even then, they got mad at you. Here's a possibility . . . Maybe you have a history with that person of using advice or giving gifts to manipulate them. You may not be aware of it. Maybe you have a history with that person of trying to control their lives and, out of love for them, manipulate them into the way you think they ought to be. If you want to know, maybe you should ask.

Because I'm a young pastor I've had lots and lots of moms ask me, "Can you talk with my son? And don't tell him we talked." It happens all the time and I'll just tell you: they know we talked. I do talk with them and I don't tell them, but trust me, they know and it bothers them.

The weird thing about the "pearls before pigs" thing is it comes from a place of love. You love that person. You care about them. You want the best for them. You want them to be happy and have a good life. Yet what you're doing is not only coming from a place of love, but a place of worry.

You know it's not a coincidence that right before this passage Jesus says, "Do not worry!" Look at the birds of the air. Look how the lilies of the field grow. Don't worry. God's going to take care of everything. He's in control. He says to seek first his kingdom and his righteousness, and all these things will be added to you. Don't worry about tomorrow. Each day has enough trouble of its own.

Jesus keeps saying, "Don't worry," and then he goes right into not judging people. And the truth is, judgment—and pearls before pigs, and sacred things before dogs—all these come from a loving place that worries about the future of this beloved person.

So, from a place of worry, you actually harm yourself. It's ironic that you're trying to help someone and you make it worse. Because you're not coming from a place that says, "You are an individual, I respect you, I believe you can make your own decisions, and I'm going to do whatever I can to help." You're saying, "You're young, and I'm old," or you're saying, "You're old and out of date, and I'm young and relevant." "I'm experienced and you're inexperienced." "You're dull and I can help you." There's this frustrating worry that, because you love this person, you are trying to help them by giving them things and giving them advice and pushing on them, but every time, all they do is go further and further away from you to where it's as if you don't even know them anymore.

How then can we help people? We walk in solidarity with them. We love them and accept them even in the midst of all the stuff we hate. We stop pushing. We've already tried that and it didn't work. We stop judging. You've already tried that, too, and it didn't work. Now it's time to love them the same way God loved you when you were a sinner, when you were broken, when you were young, and when you were naive.

Be a Companion, Not a Critic

There is something about the way Jesus helps people. Jesus invites them to his table where they are loved just as they are. He did that with Zacchaeus, a man who stole from everybody and got away with it. He did the same with Matthew, who became one of the twelve apostles. Matthew was a thief, a tax collector, and a sinner. Jesus invites him to his table and loves him. The Gospel narratives tell of many outcasts who were radically transformed because they were simply loved. Jesus doesn't pretend, he doesn't act different, he doesn't become immoral, he doesn't become a sinner, and he doesn't endorse sin or enable them—but he loves them.

Beethoven's Ninth Symphony may be the greatest musical piece ever written. It is regarded as one of the greatest masterpieces of all time, yet it was criticized. It was called a "cryptic and eccentric product of a deaf and aging composer."[2] Likewise when impressionism was born, the Salon de Paris was the main center of art criticism. This elite institution was the only way an amateur painter could become famous as an artist. The critics at the Salon initially hated impressionism. They said that Renoir's work looked as if somebody took a pistol, filled it with paint, and fired it at a canvas. These are works that are cherished and beloved today.

Do you know the names of those critics who said those things? No, neither do I. They're forgotten forever. But Beethoven's Ninth lives for the ages as perhaps the greatest work of musical composition ever. Renoir will be remembered. So will his masterpieces. Critics don't create. Critics are stuck. Judges are stuck. Creators are people who make mistakes, are messy, and take risks. Don't allow critics to bring you down, don't allow judges to bring you down, and don't become a critic or judge.

Don't be a critic; be a companion. Don't be a critic; be a creator. Be someone who loves others. You don't have to control. You don't have to convert people; that's the Holy Spirit's job. You don't have to control every outcome. You can let go and pray and be a good person and trust that God is in control. You can love people with all their sins and mistakes. Just let it go. Be free. You don't have to control. God is in control, and that's very good news.

Ask and it will be given to you; seek and you will find; knock and the door will be opened to you. For everyone who asks receives; the one who seeks finds; and to the one who knocks, the door will be opened.

Which of you, if your son asks for bread, will give him a stone? Or if he asks for a fish, will give him a snake? If you, then, though you are evil, know how to give good gifts to your children, how much more will your Father in heaven give good gifts to those who ask him! So in everything, do to others what you would have them do to you, for this sums up the Law and the Prophets.

Enter through the narrow gate. For wide is the gate and broad is the road that leads to destruction, and many enter through it. But small is the gate and narrow the road that leads to life, and only a few find it.

—Matthew 7:7–14

16 Ask, Seek, Knock

N O MATTER WHERE you are in life, no matter how hard life is getting, you should pray with shameless audacity.

Once when I was putting together a sermon on the subject of prayer I said to my teaching team, "I hope I can connect with everybody at church because I feel like I don't have any unanswered prayers." One of the students in our group, Kirstie, said, "Bobby, what about Hannah? Every time we get together, you ask us to pray for Hannah's illness." It was weird and embarrassing to me that, in thinking about unanswered prayers, I didn't think about Hannah. She has a chronic health problem that has been a mystery for years. And the reason I didn't think about it is because, even though I ask for prayer for Hannah, I believe somewhere deep down inside, somewhere on this road of praying for eight years for Hannah's healing, that God's got it under control and that our prayers have already been answered.

I wanted to begin this chapter with Hannah because, although it hasn't happened in the material world, God has confirmed deep in our hearts that this prayer is answered and that this issue is taken care of. We know that everything's going to be fine. It is part of the gift of an answered prayer—the first thing God gives you is the Holy Spirit, confidence, peace, and understanding in his presence in the midst of the storm, before the storm goes away.

When most people pray and keep praying, the goal is almost always to change the narrative somehow, to have God intervene and change the story. We could almost say that our goal in praying is to change God's mind. What actually happens when you pray for a particular outcome, as you do every day, is that *you* are the thing that changes way before the outcome. When prayer becomes a normal rhythm of your life, something happens that is deeper than just getting what you want. You get what God wants, which is much more and much better for you than what you want.

A Different Calling to Prayer

In the Sermon on the Mount, Jesus says, "Ask and it will be given to you; seek and you will find; knock and the door will be opened to you" (Matthew 7:7). This isn't a completely accurate translation, because the word "ask" is not an aorist imperative; it's a present imperative. Imperative means it's like a command. An aorist imperative would be, "Shut the door." A present imperative would be, "Always shut doors." Do you see the difference?

So to reflect the present imperative verbs, this verse would more accurately be translated as, "Keep asking and it will be given to you. Keep seeking and you will find. Keep knocking and the door will be opened." You see, that is a very different message. In our society, we want to hear, "Just ask once. Just seek once. Just knock once and the door will be opened to you."

Here Jesus is giving us a different calling to prayer. It's a call to obedience—to keep asking, keep seeking, keep praying, and never stop. There is something about praying every day, over and over for the same thing, over and over with faith, that changes you. It doesn't just change God's mind; it changes you. And that is just as important as getting what you want. In fact, prayer prepares you in case you don't get what you want, and it gets you to want different things.

God's Response to Our Prayers

Jesus then continues his teaching about prayer, saying, "Which of you, if your son asks for bread, will give him a stone? Or if he asks for a fish, will give him a snake? If you, then, though you are evil, know how to give good gifts to your children, how much more will your Father in heaven give good gifts to those who ask him!" (Matthew 7:9–11).

In other words, if your child asks you for bread, would you just hand him a rock that looks like a piece of bread? Or if he asks you for a fish, would you hand him a snake? By the way you can't even eat snakes in Judaism. So Jesus is saying, "You guys are evil. You're like wicked people compared to God, and you still do good things for your kids. Our God is the One whose love is perfect, and he is just and right in everything he does. Will he not give *his* children, whom he loves and cares for, will he not give them bread when they ask for bread? And not give them fish when they ask for fish?" Jesus makes it very, very simple. He says that God is not going to tease you by handing you a Frisbee when you ask for a pancake or poison ivy when you ask for a salad. He is going to answer, but you have to keep asking, you have to keep seeking, and you have to keep knocking because there's something about that journey that makes the end worth it.

It's interesting to see that Jesus says something very similar in Luke's recording of the Sermon on the Mount (Luke 11:1–13). He asks them, "Which of you fathers, if your son asks for a fish, will give him a snake instead? Or if he asks for an egg, will give him a scorpion? If you then, though you are evil, know how to give good gifts to your children, how much more will your Father in heaven give the Holy Spirit to those who ask him!" (vv. 11–13).

Jesus tells this story: "Suppose you have a friend, and you go to him at midnight and say, 'Friend, lend me three loaves of bread; a friend of mine on a journey has come to me, and I have no food to offer him'" (vv. 5–6). Hospitality in Jesus' day was a huge deal. It was a religious obligation to care for any visitor at your door. If a stranger came to your door and you did not offer him food and water or some kind of hospitality, it was a bad mark on your household and honor.

So, this man goes to his neighbor because he doesn't have anything to give in hospitality to a visitor. His honor is threatened. He comes to his neighbor desperate for help. It's midnight and he knocks on the door, but the neighbor doesn't come down. He gets desperate. The neighbor says, "Don't bother me. The door is already locked, and my children and I are in bed. I can't get up and give you anything" (v. 7).

Jesus tells us, even though the neighbor will not get up and give the bread because of friendship, he will surely get up and give him as much as he needs because of the shameless audacity of the request (v. 8).

The neighbor demonstrates "shameless audacity" to keep knocking (v. 8), in his underwear, on the door at midnight, shouting, "I need food! I need to be hospitable. I will not put my family's name at risk. Please, give me bread. Give me something to give in hospitality."

And the neighbor says, "No, go away."

The man says, "I won't go away! Answer the door!"

And the neighbor says, "No, go away."

Then the man says, "I won't go away! I need bread! I need it!" Shameless audacity.

Jesus said that surely the wicked neighbor would come and answer the door in response to such shameless audacity. "If you then, though you are evil, know how to give good gifts to your children, how much more will your Father in heaven give the Holy Spirit to those who ask him!" (v. 13). These are the words of Jesus, God incarnate, who knows the Father. He is revealing to us the kind of God we serve: a God who responds to his people, but also a God who calls his people to pray.

Prayer Changes Things

I read about an interesting study that showed how prayer changes things. In Dallas Willard's great work, *The Divine Conspiracy*, he describes a study from a cardiologist at the University of California San Francisco named Randolph Byrd. It was published in 1988. Byrd did a randomized double-blind study. He was the head of a cardiology department at a hospital, and under his care were 393 patients. He decided to do a study about how prayer affects health. So he had three different churches pray for half of his patients. He kept all of his data on the patients, how they were doing. In the study, 192 people were prayed for, and 201 people were not prayed for. That functioned as a control group.

For the first group, the one being prayed for, Bird simply gave their first name and the first letter of their last name to Bible studies and churches. The patients who were being prayed for had no idea. The second blind was that the doctors treating the patients also had no idea that the patients were being prayed for.

The group that was prayed for was five times less likely to need antibiotics and three times less likely to develop pulmonary edema (lungs filling with fluid). None of the group needed life support, whereas twenty-three in the other group did. And significantly fewer died—only three in the group that were prayed for, compared to thirty or forty in the other group who died. Now, this was an amazing finding because something was happening spiritually that was affecting their material world. Some of them still died. Some of them still needed antibiotics. So it wasn't perfect, but yet you see that it changed the group that was being prayed for.[1]

There was a critic named William Harris who questioned this, and this made it even better. He decided that he wanted to do a continuous weighted system. He redid the same study in a different group, and Harris concluded that supplementary remote blinded intercessory prayer produced a measureable improvement in medical outcomes of critically ill patients.[2] William Nolan, MD, published in the *Skeptical Inquirer*, "It sounds like this study will stand up against scrutiny. Maybe we doctors ought to be writing on our order sheets, 'Pray three times a day.' Heck, if it works, it works."[3]

The Mystery of Prayer

Why does God wait? Why doesn't God just give us what we want now if he loves us? It may be that God wants to give you more than what you are praying for. You are praying for a cure for your body, but it may be that God also wants to give you healing in your soul. You are praying for your child to come to Christ, but it may be that God wants you to come to Christ in a new way. You are praying for financial breakthrough, but it may be that God wants to purge your life of idolatry as well. It may be that God doesn't want to give you what you want until you want something else in his kingdom first.

In order to understand prayer, we have to be okay with mystery because we are dealing with a spiritual realm our minds can't comprehend fully. We don't have to understand it, but we do have to know it works. I have no idea how to program a computer, but I know how to surf the Internet. I have no idea how to fix my car, but I know how to drive it. You don't need to understand everything about prayer in order to make prayer work; you just have to understand that it works. And you don't have to understand when your prayer is going to become a breakthrough; you just have to know you will have a breakthrough. You have to stay obedient to what God says, which is, "Keep praying, keep asking, keep knocking."

Life is challenging. Life is difficult. But life is eternal and spiritual and it follows a certain set of rules. I am calling you to pray to a God who lives outside of the book of history. Who writes the book and is writing it now and has already written and can change it. To pray to him, your Dad in heaven who loves you and was there when you were born, and will be there to catch your breath when you die. Pray to him and keep praying. Keep asking. Keep seeking him. Keep knocking on his door because he will answer.

The Golden Rule

There are few ideas more famous than "do to others what you would have them do to you" (Matthew 7:12). Believe it or not, Jesus didn't pull this idea extemporaneously out of the sky. It was a play off of an older saying already in existence now called "the Silver Rule." Though we are unsure where exactly this Silver Rule came from, we do know it existed when Jesus said the Golden Rule. The Silver Rule stated, "Don't do to others what you wouldn't want them to do to you." This "cause no harm" idea was very prevalent in first-century Judaism. Unfortunately, the idea became a license to hold others in contempt and not aid those in need. Jesus challenges the idea by removing the "don't" in the Silver Rule, effectively making the command to be proactive in your love and care rather than passive, disconnected, and uninterested.

In the famous story of the Good Samaritan (Luke 10), Jesus makes the idea even more poignant. In this story, a man has been robbed and beaten nearly to death. Two religious figures, first a priest and next a Levite, do nothing to help the poor fellow. They simply walk by him. Finally, the hero of the story, the Samaritan, rescues the man and pays to have him brought to full health. Samaritans were a group of people who were hated by religious Jews. Here, however, Jesus shows the Samaritan to be more righteous than the priest and Levite because he lived the Golden Rule rather than the Silver Rule.

Jesus says the Golden Rule "sums up the Law and the Prophets" when we are proactive to care for human good. You see, if you only follow the idea of "cause no harm," then you will never go out of your place of comfort to help others and bring an end to the kingdom of darkness in our world.

No Neutrality with Jesus

Jesus is polarizing. Jesus is either/or. Peter Kreeft asks, "Why is Jesus the most embarrassing name in the world?"[4] Think about that. If you disagree with that, just talk about Jesus in a secular or academic setting. You get in those settings and you can talk about Buddha. You can talk about Moses, Mohammed, and whomever. You can talk about great prophets and great leaders, but there's something different about talking about Jesus.

Kreeft tells us that talking about Jesus is similar to talking about sex. When you talk about sex, there is no *neutral* language. It's a language of intimacy, love, and romance that stirs the heart. Or it's vulgar, offensive, and crudely funny. Or it's scientific, technical, medical language that holds it far away, sterile.

We do that same thing with Jesus. We talk about Jesus as deeply intimate and heart moving. Or it's vulgar if using his name to curse or to swear. Or we use some kind of technical, theological language to hold him at a distance. That's because Jesus stirs the heart, the emotions, the will, and the mind. His name itself has spiritual power and that's why it cannot even be mentioned in a neutral way. To say "Jesus" anywhere moves everything. Millions of people have spent trillions of hours writing and making art and worshipping and lifting up this name. There is no name like Jesus.

And the name of Jesus causes you to make a choice. Everyone who followed Jesus when he was on earth seemed to go in one of two directions. Either they wanted to worship him and follow him and be with him and hang on his every word, or they wanted to kill him and crucify him and plot against him and see him dead.

No one could be neutral with Jesus then, and no one can be neutral with Jesus today. There is no middle road with him. There is no neutral. There is no lukewarm. There's yes or there's no. There's a narrow and difficult road or a wide and easy road. One leads to life, and the other leads to death. There is no middle ground. Jesus demands everything or nothing. His name has power, and every time his name is mentioned, your soul is reminded of a choice you have yet to make: *Will I do what he said? Or will I do what I say?*

There is a narrow gate and difficult road—and there is a wide gate and easy road. Jesus says many people will go the easy way that leads to destruction and few will take the hard way that leads to life. We want to be careful not to make this passage about heaven and hell. We know based on a comprehensive understanding of the gospel that going to heaven isn't about "doing good." Rather this passage is about having a life that matters, that is happy, and that is meaningful to God. Having that kind of life is not easy, and it's not obvious, but it's worth it.

This is good wisdom for life in general. Few great things in life come easy or free. Even when they do, we tend to not value them in the way we do when we work hard and pay the price for them. You can't have resurrection without the cross. Jesus is showing us that if we want to be full of life, then we have to be willing to do the difficult things of being a disciple. He does not promise the happy kingdom life to be easy, but he does promise it to be worth it.

Watch out for false prophets. They come to you in sheep's clothing, but inwardly they are ferocious wolves. By their fruit you will recognize them. Do people pick grapes from thornbushes, or figs from thistles? Likewise, every good tree bears good fruit, but a bad tree bears bad fruit. A good tree cannot bear bad fruit, and a bad tree cannot bear good fruit. Every tree that does not bear good fruit is cut down and thrown into the fire. Thus, by their fruit you will recognize them.

Not everyone who says to me, "Lord, Lord," will enter the kingdom of heaven, but only the one who does the will of my Father who is in heaven. Many will say to me on that day, "Lord, Lord, did we not prophesy in your name and in your name drive out demons and in your name perform many miracles?" Then I will tell them plainly, "I never knew you. Away from me, you evildoers!"

—Matthew 7:15–23

17 Bearing the Fruit of the Spirit

E VERYONE IN LEADERSHIP struggles to live up to the expectations of those who follow. Pastors and ministers are rarely very good at doing what they tell everyone else to do. In some ways, this is okay. "You should practice what you preach" is a good axiom because practice doesn't imply that you have to be perfect. You don't have to be perfect at what you preach, but you have to be working on it. You can't be perfect, you're not going to get everything right, but your life should be bearing the fruit of what you claim to believe. If you believe we serve a big God, your life ought to reflect a faith in a big God.

We are meant to practice what we preach, even though we don't necessarily perfect it.

Recognize False Teachers by Their Fruit

In the Sermon on the Mount Jesus says, "Watch out for false prophets. They come to you in sheep's clothing, but inwardly they are ferocious wolves" (Matthew 7:15). This means they want to devour you. They want to use you.

> "By their fruit you will recognize them. Do people pick grapes from thornbushes, or figs from thistles? Likewise, every good tree bears good fruit, but a bad tree bears bad fruit. A good tree cannot bear bad fruit, and a bad tree cannot bear good fruit. Every tree that does not bear good fruit is cut down and thrown into the fire. Thus, by their fruit you will recognize them" (vv. 16–20).

Though we may not recognize them, there are people who are influencing and pouring into our lives. Some will influence us in the ways of Jesus, and others will influence us away from the ways of Jesus. Jesus tells us we need to discern the difference between these two. The way we can discern the difference is by examining their fruit. "By their fruit you will recognize them."

When Paul writes to the Galatian church about the fruit of the Spirit, he is referring to this particular saying found in the Sermon on the Mount where Jesus is describing "bearing fruit." Paul says this fruit looks like this: "love, joy, peace, forbearance, kindness, goodness, faithfulness, gentleness and self-control" (Galatians 5:22–23). The Holy Spirit yields this fruit in the life of the disciple—the same fruit Jesus yielded in his ministry.

Do They Remind You of Jesus?

Here is the question posed to us by Jesus: "The people who are speaking into your life, do they remind you of me? Do they look like me in the way they act and the choices they make? The way they treat their neighbor? Do you want to be more like them? If you were more like them, if you emulated their lives, if you acted like them, if you bore the same kind of fruit they bear, would you be a better person for doing so?"

You see, many of us admire people in our lives because they're so wealthy or so successful, such great communicators, so attractive or charismatic. But what kind of fruit are they bearing? Are they loving and joy-filled, peaceful, patient people? "Well, no," you say. "They're kind of grumpy, legalistic, angry, vindictive, gossiping, greedy, lying. But they're quite interesting."

Listen, if you want to be more charismatic but also be shallower, follow those people and then you'll bear their fruit. But if you want to be like Jesus, if you want to live a life that bears fruit, if you truly want to be a difference maker, then follow people who bear real fruit. By their fruit, you will know them.

Two Deceptions about Spiritual Fruit

When we talk about spiritual fruit, there are two great deceptions. The first deception comes from the world and the second deception usually comes from the church. The first great deception is that you are an apple tree even though you bear thistles. We hear this often. "My life is a mess, I'm lost, I'm confused, I make all the wrong decisions, I continue to hurt people and be completely self-centered."

"You're okay. So am I."

"But my life is bearing thistles."

"Trust me. You're an apple tree."

That deception will always keep you a thistle tree and you'll always bear needles and brambles. This is a major problem in the world today. We walk away from what is actually true to what we want to be true. We want to be apple bearers, but we're not. We are fruitless because of egotism and self-deception.

We believe the way to become apple bearers is just to say to ourselves a bunch of times: "I'm an apple bearer. I'm an apple bearer," even though we treat our neighbors with contempt.

And we're hurried.

And our lives are cluttered.

And we feel lost.

And we're living every day in quiet desperation.

"I'm an apple bearer, I'm an apple bearer." This lie will get you nowhere.

The second great deception is often in the church, and this is something that bothers me tremendously because I know this has wounded many. It is the opposite of the first deception. The second deception is that you are a thistle tree even though you bear apples. Your life bears tremendous fruit, you love your neighbor, you're growing, you're thriving, and people say you're a bad person. "You're horrible. You're no good. You'll always be like that." When you mess up, people say, "I

knew you would do that because that's what you always do."
Your life is bearing figs and grapes and fruit, and they say you
are a thistle bearer. That's the other great lie. Both lies will
keep you trapped.

Accurately Assess Spiritual Fruit

Begin by being a realist. If you're a thistle tree, be a thistle tree.
Own it. And if you're an apple bearer, own that too. This is the
way you become a fruit bearer.

You become a fruit bearer by claiming and acknowledging that you are a thistle bush and there is nothing you can
do about it. That is the gospel. The gospel comes to the man
or woman who says, "Lord, I am a thistle-bearing, dry, dead
bush and I can do nothing about it. Help! In my very DNA,
I will bear thistles and needles and hurt people, then never
bear fruit. In my very DNA, I am harming my neighbor.
Help me! I am desperate. I need you! I try harder and harder
and do worse. Help!" That's how the gospel begins, because
God then comes to that person—the thistle-bearing, thorny,
dried-out bush—and he cuts it at the root. Rips it out of the
ground violently. Then preciously carries that branch to a
vine and he grafts it onto the vine in his own special way.

Now that thistle branch feels something new. It feels
something new in its branches. It feels a new kind of sap.
A new kind of green comes over it. A new kind of leaf and
blossom begins to form. And, as it abides in this vine, it starts
to bear real fruit. Not because it's trying harder, but because
in that moment of total emptiness, lostness, sin, depravity,
wickedness, and shame, it cries out to a loving God who kills

it and grafts it to something beautiful and wonderful—to Jesus. That's the gospel. The gospel does not say you are good when you are wicked. The gospel does not say you are wicked when you are good. The gospel says we all begin as thistle trees but need to die and be grafted to a vine so that we each become a branch.

Meno with Jesus

Jesus is the vine, God is the vinedresser, and the Holy Spirit is the sap.

Jesus says in John 15 that if we abide in the vine, then we will bear fruit. "I am the vine; you are the branches. If you remain in me and I in you, you will bear much fruit; apart from me you can do nothing" (v. 5). The word he uses for "remain" or "abide" in this verse is a Greek word, *meno*. It means to make your home in something. *Meno* is more than abiding. It's finding comfort in a haven of rest.

Meno looks like this: I remember back when I was a child, our family would visit the mountains. There is something wonderful about coming out of the snow and going into a cabin. You sit down by the fire and everything on you is wet. The best part is the wet socks. You sit back and the wet socks don't come off easily; they peel off, and it feels good. You lay that wet sock by the fire, then the other one, and you kick up your bare feet. They're freezing, but they start to thaw and dry, and you lean back in the chair. You are "*meno*-ing." You are finding a home, a cabin in the snow—a warm, comfortable place of well-being. Jesus wants us to *meno* in his life and presence. Find your place in him. He wants to be your cabin in the woods. Do that and you will bear fruit.

If you don't understand the idea of abiding in Jesus, then do this: always do the next right thing. You get good at things when you practice them, not when you read about them or talk about them. If I were to need heart surgery, I would not want the surgeon to come in and say, "I'm going to be honest with you. I've never done a surgery before, but I have read every book, magazine, and article there is to know about heart surgery. I know more than anybody does. Trust me." If he's never done it I'm certainly not going to let him start on me. God doesn't want Christians like that either. Do the next right thing today. Begin practicing.

Do the Will of the Father

Jesus says in Matthew 7:21, "Not everyone who says to me 'Lord, Lord,' will enter the kingdom of heaven, but only the one who does the will of my Father who is in heaven." *Only the one who does the will of my Father*. He continues, "Many will say to me on that day, 'Lord, Lord, did we not prophesy in your name and in your name drive out demons and in your name perform many miracles?' Then I will tell them plainly, 'I never knew you. Away from me, you evildoers!'" (vv. 22–23).

How many churchgoers do you think will be surprised when they stand before God and they say, "Lord, Lord," and they think that's going to get them into heaven, and they realize it doesn't?

I like to think of these people as password Christians who follow password theology. "Let me get you in a room, guys. I'm going to let you in on the password. You have the password; you're going to get in. The password is to say, 'Lord, Lord' to Jesus. If you do that, you're good."

Now, especially if you grew up in the church, this passage can make you feel a bit insecure because you maybe have not read this passage, or read it in this light, before. But think about how often churches teach that if you simply pray this prayer, you will go to heaven. If you simply say, "Lord, Lord," and nothing else changes in your life, you will enter the kingdom of God. Jesus addresses that idea specifically when he says, "Many will say to me on that day, 'Lord, Lord,' and I will say, 'Get away from me. I never knew you.'" Uh-oh.

So there's the first group he talks about, password Christians, and then the second group he talks about are spiritual-firework Christians. He specifically mentions people who can heal the sick and people who can raise the dead and people who can speak prophecies into others' lives. They'll say, "Lord, didn't we do all these things? We cast out demons and worked many miracles. We did all of these great things," and Jesus will say, "Depart from me. I never knew you."

When Jesus is talking in the Sermon on the Mount about a person saying, "Lord, Lord," the word *Lord* does not mean "God" (though Jesus is God). *Lord* means that if Jesus is your Lord, then he's your boss. He's your master. He's your ruler. He's your king. What Jesus wants, Jesus gets, and that's what it means for Jesus to be Lord of your life. It doesn't mean you say it. It means that your life follows what you claim to be true.

Do the Right Thing

We rationalize and justify the wrong things we do in life. It's amazing to me that a thief always blames the victim. "She shouldn't have left her car unlocked," he says. "He shouldn't have left his wallet so far out. If I didn't take it, somebody else would have." That's what we do when we take a shirt from the store and leave the tag on intending to return it the next day after wearing it to the party. That's what we do when we steal music from the Internet or software for our business. The things we do that we know are wrong, we will find a way to justify. Too often we don't want to actually be good. We only want to feel like we are good.

If we as Christians want the world to take us seriously in what we claim to be true, then we need to do what is right and not do what is wrong. It's just that simple. We need to be people who bear fruit. I don't mean a new kind of legalism. I mean spiritual fruit. I mean people who clearly show the love and life and goodness and sap of the Holy Spirit in life, people who abide so deeply in God's presence they don't even desire their old ways. It's not even something they care about anymore.

It's even amazing that the things we want for our children are not the things we want for ourselves. We say, "I want my kids to be moral. I want my kids to do the right thing. I want them to get an education. I want them to be happily married. I want them to do all of these productive, healthy, positive things." Yet we don't want it for ourselves or model it for our children.

Jesus was talking to farmers when he was saying, "You will recognize them by their fruit." When I lived in Oklahoma, I loved farmers. Farmers just have a way of seeing the world that is right. I used to go fishing with my buddies in the summer. We would go out to these farms in the woods. We were in Oklahoma, close to the Ozarks. There were lots of trees and hills. We'd knock on someone's door, a farmer would answer the door, and I'd ask, "Can we go fishing in your pond?"

The farmer would look me up and down, and he'd say, "You're a good man. You can fish on my land." Somehow he just intuitively knew I was not going to harm his land. The farmer sees the world in a way that's simple.

That's what Jesus wants from us. He wants us, very simply, to measure the people who are speaking into our lives by their fruit. To surround yourself with people who bear fruit, people who live their lives obviously as fruit bearers. Don't be tricked by people who speak well and are attractive but are grumpy, angry, legalistic, selfish, vain, or greedy when few are looking. Surround yourself with people who remind you of Jesus, and then become that kind of person.

•••••••••••••••••••••••••••••••••

Therefore everyone who hears these words of mine and puts them into practice is like a wise man who built his house on the rock. The rain came down, the streams rose, and the winds blew and beat against that house; yet it did not fall, because it had its foundation on the rock. But everyone who hears these words of mine and does not put them into practice is like a foolish man who built his house on sand. The rain came down, the streams rose, and the winds blew and beat against that house, and it fell with a great crash.

—Matthew 7:24–27

•••••••••••••••••••••••••••••••••

18 Build It on the Rock

J ESUS FINISHES HIS Sermon on the Mount with something like, "Now, go do what I just told you to do."

That may seem simple, but it is actually a big deal. Christians sometimes don't like to do things. Jesus is essentially saying, "Stop talking about it, stop studying it, and stop thinking about it. Stop being cerebral. Just get out there and go do what I told you to do." He says that if you do this, your life will be like a house that's built on the rock.

As I'm writing this we just had a big storm come through California, deemed Pineapple Express. These last four days we've been getting huge storms. Wednesday was really dramatic. Wednesday evening there were rain and mudslides. I was on my couch reading by the fire and just enjoying it. The next morning I headed off to spend my day in prayer at a retreat center. The rain was coming down hard; it was pouring. When I arrived there, I parked in the top lot of the church that owns this retreat center. The first thing I noticed was that all of these really nice tents and other things that had been left outside had been demolished from the wind and the rain. My heart really went out to all these people. But I thought, *That's what Californians do.*

That's what happens when you live in a state where, during winter, spring, summer, and fall, it is 72 degrees and sunny 99 percent of the time. You are not ready for that storm when it comes through. And even though they tell you a storm is coming, a storm is blowing, Californians just don't think in terms of bad weather. It's not something that factors in for us. You turn on the evening news and Monday through Friday, it's just pictures of the sun going across the screen.

Now, I spent six years living in an opposite type of world. I lived in Oklahoma in a town called Broken Arrow, just outside of Tulsa, and it has the worst weather in the whole world. Even on beautiful days, it's always windy. And there's something about Oklahomans who, in contrast, are very different from Californians. They are always ready for bad weather. They're always interested in the weather. They're always thinking about weather. If you go to a Starbucks in Tulsa, you will see people on their laptops looking at the weather forecast, and not just in their own town. They're thinking, *That's interesting. Let's see what kind of weather is going on in Michigan. Oh, that's interesting.* People in Oklahoma are obsessed with the weather.

The reason I say this is that since people in Oklahoma are obsessed about the weather, they're always prepared for it. They have shelters. They have well-built homes. They're ready for the wind. They are never going to leave an expensive tent outside and allow it to be demolished by the weather. That would never happen in Oklahoma. The tent would be safely cleaned, wrapped, and placed in the shed where it belongs. And that's the big difference in the Midwest.

I still remember the time I saw my first tornado. I was a California boy really scared of extreme weather. I was staying at a guy's house before I spoke at a local Baptist college. We were eating at the dinner table and nobody was paying attention. The pastor, his family, and another guy who was traveling with me were eating while . . . *boom, boom, boom, boom, boom!* The thunder outside sounded like bombs falling. All the while, I was eating my food and looking around to see that nobody else was even paying attention to the winds blowing, the rains coming. Then all of a sudden, it all stopped. The pastor looked up and said, "Uh-oh." He went outside to check that everything was in the shelter, and he came back in saying, "You know what, fellas, don't worry about it. There isn't going to be any tornado. There are no tornado sirens." Then, almost as if we were in a movie, immediately we heard a siren and a police car went speeding down the road as the wind blew and howled. Of course, what did we three wise gentlemen do? We walked out on the porch to see the tornado. It actually wasn't that big a deal. We could see a tornado; it looked like a little finger spinning and then it moved quickly off in the distance and disappeared.

But my host wasn't afraid of a tornado and he wasn't afraid of the storm. Why? He was prepared. We might say that he anticipated the rains coming, the winds blowing, the streams rising. And as an Oklahoman, he was ready for it. His stuff wasn't destroyed, his house wasn't trashed, and his life was not in danger because he was ready for the storm.

Our lives are like this. Some of us are ready for the storms of life and others of us are not. Building your life in the storm means you do what Jesus tells you to do. Jesus wants disciples. That's something we Christians so easily forget. Jesus actually wants us to do the things he tells us to do. Jesus wants disciples, and he wants us to obey. He doesn't want us to obey because he's arrogant, because he's angry, because he's controlling, or because he's manipulative. He wants us to obey because he loves us.

Are You Building Your House on the Rock?

Jesus says, "Therefore, everyone who hears these words of mine and puts them into practice is like a wise man who built his house on the rock. The rain came down, the streams rose, and the winds blew and beat against that house, yet it did not fall, because it had its foundation on the rock. But everyone who hears these words of mine and does not put them into practice is like a foolish man who built his house on sand. The rain came down, the streams rose, and the winds blew and beat against that house, and it fell with a great crash" (Matthew 7:24–27).

The rains are coming. The wind will be blowing. The streams will be rising. Are you ready? Whether you're a Christian or not, there is going to be wind, there is going to be rain, there are going to be rising streams. And the only way you will make it, the only way your life will be something of true eternal value, the only way it will actually have meaning is if you follow the master of living, who is Jesus. If you do what Jesus says, then your life will be strong, steadfast, anchored to the rock, immovable, and unshakeable.

Imagine a bunch of people settling on an island. After landing on the island, all these settlers go down by the river where they don't have to walk far to get fish or fresh water. It's the most convenient place to have a settlement. One smart man puts his house upon the hill where the rock is. And he has to walk every day. It's really hard. He has to take those buckets down to fill with water and bring them back up to his house. He has to go a long way to get his food and his fish. He tells those people who have settled near the water, "This is a rainy place, this is a windy place, and you are too close to that river."

The people ignore him and say, "Oh, you fool. Look how easy our life is and look how hard your life is up there on the rock."

And he says, "My friends, the winds are coming, the rain's coming, the streams will be rising." Sure enough, the storm comes and all those people who had that easy life down by the river, it was all for nothing. It was all destroyed. That's what life is like.

If you've built a house on the rock, then the storms can't harm you. You don't have to worry about the storms of life because you have taken the time to build your house, your life, the right way.

The Knowing-Doing Gap

A study from Stanford University shows many companies have this thing called the knowing-doing gap.[1] These companies get consultants to come in, to teach them something about customer service, for example. This company knows they need to improve customer service, so they host a customer-service seminar with a customer-service consultant. And they get new customer-service technology. They write customer service into their values for their company. And they have all of this knowledge about what the best and newest trends are in customer service. And then nothing happens. This knowing-doing gap happens all the time in businesses. All of this money and time is thrown at learning, and yet customer service just never actually happens. This happens all the time in the church—and in our lives as believers.

We spend enough time looking at the original languages, going to Bible studies, and listening to podcasts. Maybe it's time to stop listening and start doing. We are so smart. We can make the greatest arguments. We can tell you everything theologically and doctrinally about Jesus. Do something! I feel like he says, "Many pastors and theologians and many seminary professors and many spiritual people will say to me on that day, 'We knew lots of stuff about you. We know you're Lord.' And I will say, 'Just get away from me. I don't even know you. You didn't do anything I told you to do. Just go away.'" What you know really almost doesn't matter, to some degree, unless you put it into practice.

We love to talk. Talking is a way of procrastinating. Did you know that? It's a way to feel good about delaying making a choice. Talking almost feels like doing. It's not. We want to be "vampire Christians," as Dallas Willard put it.[2] We want Jesus just for a little bit of blood. That's it. We want his blood and then nothing else, and so we walk like the undead. But Jesus doesn't allow that.

This Is Your Chance!

Jesus is calling you to stop being so much of a talker and be much more of a doer. It's time to do something this week. Something is going to present itself to you in which you have a chance to do the things we've spent this whole book studying. You will actually have the opportunity to do something Jesus told you to do. There will be a couple next door who is poor and needs babysitting and money for movies and dinner, and what you are going to say?

Say, "This is my chance!"

You're going to be at the pharmacy waiting for your medication, and some guy is going to cut in line in front of you.

"This is my chance!"

Yes! It's your chance to love that guy and encourage him. He's sick and he needs help.

You're going to have a dear friend who's in the hospital and you're going to be busy and you're not going to know when to find the time.

"This is my chance."

Somebody's going to lash out at you in anger.

"This is my chance."

Every day is an opportunity to do what Jesus taught. It's never easy but always fulfilling. Jesus has a way of living.

He wants us to be the light of the world.

He wants us to relent from our anger.

He wants us to put our family first.

He wants us to stop lying.

He wants us to love our enemies.

He wants us to care for those who speak badly about us.

He wants to care for the needy, those who are hungry, those who are thirsty.

He wants us to care about justice and not to do it for our own glory, but to do it for others.

He wants us to be praying people, who pray simply, and pray because we know that God is listening.

He wants us to be fasting people.

He wants us to be people who stop worrying, who don't think with concern about tomorrow or regret yesterday, but live today in the easy rhythms of grace.

He wants us not to store up for ourselves treasures on earth where moths and rust destroy, but to store up real heavenly treasure that we can access today, that never goes away.

He wants us to stop judging people, to stop shoving religion down people's throats.

He wants us to know that if we need something, we can ask him.

Jesus is going to come. He's going to deliver. We know that we serve a good God. There is a way of living and a way of doing, and we're going to do it.

Notes

Introduction: A New Day, a New Person

1. Virginia Stem Owens, "God and Man at Texas A&M," *Reformed Journal* 37, no. 11 (1987): 3–4.

2. Dallas Willard, *The Divine Conspiracy: Rediscovering Our Hidden Life in God* (San Francisco: Harper San Francisco, 1998).

Chapter 2: Salty Do-Gooders

1. Joel Lovell, "George Saunders's Advice to Graduates," *The 6th Floor* (blog), *New York Times*, July 31, 2013, http://6th-floor.blogs.nytimes.com/2013/07/31/george-saunderss-advice-to-graduates/.

2. Dwight Edwards, *Releasing the Rivers Within: The Exhilaration of Utter Dependence on God* (Colorado Springs: WaterBrook, 2003), 31.

3. Roger Austin, *I'd Like to Die, but I've Got Stuff to Do: Helpful Hints for Victorious Living* (Pittsburgh: RoseDog Books, 2012), 75.

4. Deborah DeFord, Judy Speicher, and Mark LaFlaur, eds., *"Quotable" Quotes: Wit and Wisdom for Every Occasion*

from America's Most Popular Magazine (Pleasantville, NY: Reader's Digest, 1997) 43.

Chapter 3: The Rabbi's Yoke

1. William Barclay, *The Gospel of Matthew*, vol. 1, The Daily Study Bible, rev. ed. (Philadelphia: Westminster, 1975), 127.

Chapter 4: Anger Is Like a Headache

1. Bill Gaultiere, "Dallas Willard's Definitions," Soul Shepherding for You and Your Ministry, May 28, 2013, http://www.soulshepherding.org/2013/05/dallas-willards-definitions/.

2. Dallas Willard, *The Divine Conspiracy: Rediscovering Our Hidden Life in God* (San Francisco: HarperSanFrancisco, 1998), 135, 150–51.

Chapter 5: Missing the Mark

1. Søren Kierkegaard, *Purity of Heart Is to Will One Thing: Spiritual Preparation for the Office of Confession*, trans. Douglas V. Steere (New York: Harper, 1956).

2. Ronald Rolheiser, *The Holy Longing: The Search for a Christian Spirituality* (New York: Doubleday, 1999).

3. Dennis Prager, *Happiness Is a Serious Problem: A Human Nature Repair Manual* (New York: Regan, 1998), 32.

Chapter 7: The Honest, Easy Life

1. Robert S. Feldman, *The Liar in Your Life: The Way to Truthful Relationships* (New York: Twelve / Grand Central, 2009), 14.

2. Fyodor Dostoyevsky, *The Brothers Karamazov: A Novel in Four Parts with Epilogue*, trans. Richard Pevear and Larissa Volokhonsky (San Francisco: North Point, 1990), 58.

Chapter 8: Courageous Peacemakers

1. Eugene H. Peterson, *Christ Plays in Ten Thousand Places: A Conversation in Spiritual Theology* (Grand Rapids: Eerdmans, 2005), 136.
2. I am indebted to John Ortberg's teachings throughout this book. Podcasts of his insightful sermons at Menlo Park Presbyterian Church can be found at https://itunes.apple.com/us/podcast/menlo-park-presbyterian-church/id129950807?mt=2.

Chapter 9: Unstoppable Love

1. Dallas Willard, quoted in Bill Gaultiere, "Jesus Jujitsu: The Power to Turn the Other Cheek," Soul Shepherding for You and Your Ministry, August 13, 2005, http://www.soulshepherding.org/2005/08/jesus-jujitsu-the-power-to-turn-the-other-cheek/.

Chapter 10: Secretly Good

1. Dan Allender, "Suffer the Kindness," Kingdom series, sermon delivered at Mars Hill Bible Church, Grand Rapids, MI, October 10, 2010, podcast, http://marshill.org/teaching/2010/10/10/suffer-the-kindness/.
2. Jonah Berger, *Contagious: Why Things Catch On* (New York: Simon & Schuster, 2013), 29–31.

3. Henri J. M. Nouwen, *Life of the Beloved: Spiritual Living in a Secular World* (New York: Crossroad, 1992).

Chapter 12: Feasting on the Spirit

1. "Brennan Manning Live at Woodcrest," YouTube, uploaded May 30, 2007, https://www.youtube.com/watch?v=pQi_IDV2bgM.

2. Brennan Manning, *The Ragamuffin Gospel Visual Edition: Good News for the Bedraggled, Beat-Up, and Burnt Out* (Sisters, OR: Multnomah, 2005), 36.

Chapter 14: Birds and Lillies

1. Reata Strickland, ed., *Interview with God* (New York: Free Press, 2001).

Chapter 15: Letting Go of Self-Righteousness

1. Naomi Gordon, "'You've the Personality of a Handle': 17 of Simon Cowell's best insults," Digital Spy, October 7, 2013, http://www.digitalspy.com/celebrity/s103/the-x-factor/best-in-showbiz/a521604/.

2. Nicholas Cook, *Beethoven Symphony No. 9* (Cambridge: Cambridge University Press, 1993), back cover.

Chapter 16: Ask, Seek, Knock

1. Dallas Willard, *The Divine Conspiracy: Recovering Our Hidden Life in God* (New York: HarperCollins, 1998), 248; Larry Dossey, *Healing Words: The Power of Prayer and the Practice of Medicine* (New York: HarperCollins, 1993), 179–81.

2. William S. Harris et al., "A Randomized, Controlled Trial of the Effects of Remote, Intercessory Prayer on Outcomes in Patients Admitted to the Coronary Care Unit," *Archives of Internal Medicine* 159, no. 19 (October 25, 1999): 2273–78, doi:10.1001/archinte.159.19.2273.
3. William Nolan, quoted in Dossey, *Healing Words*, 180.
4. Peter Kreeft, *Jesus-Shock* (South Bend, IN: St. Augustines Press, 2008).

Chapter 18: Build It on the Rock

1. Jeffrey Pfeffer, "The Knowing-Doing Gap," *Insights*, Stanford Graduate School of Business, November 1, 1999, http://www.gsb.stanford.edu/insights/knowing-doing-gap.
2. Dallas Willard, *The Great Omission: Reclaiming Jesus's Essential Teachings on Discipleship* (San Francisco: Harper-San Francisco, 2006).

About the Author

BOBBY SCHULLER IS a pastor, writer, and speaker on the internationally broadcast television program *The Hour of Power*. He is the grandson of Robert H. Schuller, founder of the Crystal Cathedral. Along with hosting *The Hour of Power*, he is senior pastor of Shepherd's Grove church in Garden Grove, California—the congregation formerly known as the Crystal Cathedral. He has a passion for using media to engage the most distracted culture in history and believes the power of God can answer the most challenging questions facing today's generation.

Bobby received his Master of Divinity degree from Fuller Theological Seminary. He resides in Orange, California, with his wife, Hannah, and their children, Haven and Cohen.

WORTHY
PUBLISHING

If you enjoyed this book, will you consider sharing the message with others?

- Mention the book in a Facebook post, Twitter update, Pinterest pin, blog post, or upload a picture through Instagram.

- Recommend this book to those in your small group, book club, workplace, and classes.

- Head over to facebook.com/worthypublishing, "LIKE" the page, and post a comment as to what you enjoyed the most.

- Tweet "I recommend reading #HappinessAccordingtoJesus by @BobbySchuller // @worthypub"

- Pick up a copy for someone you know who would be challenged and encouraged by this message.

- Write a book review online.

You can subscribe to Worthy Publishing's newsletter at worthypublishing.com.

WORTHY PUBLISHING
FACEBOOK PAGE

WORTHY PUBLISHING
WEBSITE

Would you like to receive a free audio CD of a *Sermon on the Mount* message delivered in the 1970s by Pastor Bobby's grandfather, Dr. Robert H. Schuller? Limited supply. One per address. Please allow 4-6 weeks for delivery.

NAME

ADDRESS

CITY

STATE   ZIP

MAIL TO:
HOUR OF POWER
PO BOX 100, GARDEN GROVE
CALIFORNIA, 92842-0100

OR CALL:
1-866-GET-HOPE (438-4673)